ST PAUL'S BIBLIOGRAPHIES 11

A BIBLIOGRAPHY OF
EDWARD JENNER

# ST PAUL'S BIBLIOGRAPHIES

Forthcoming titles of related interest

*British Anatomy 1525–1800: a bibliography*
Revised edition, by K. F. Russell

*Bibliography of Dr William Harvey*
Sir Geoffrey Keynes
Third edition, revised by Dr G. Whitteridge

*Bio-Bibliography of Vesalius*
Harvey Cushing
Reissue with new introduction

Edward Jenner. Engraved by W. Read from a drawing.

# A BIBLIOGRAPHY OF
# EDWARD JENNER

*by*
WILLIAM LeFANU

SECOND EDITION

ST PAUL'S BIBLIOGRAPHIES
1985

# ST PAUL'S BIBLIOGRAPHIES 11

First published in 1951 as
*A Bio-Bibliography of Edward Jenner*,
this second edition, revised and
reset, and entitled *A Bibliography of
Edward Jenner* is published by St
Paul's Bibliographies, West End
House, 1 Step Terrace,
Winchester, Hampshire SO22 5BW,
England.

British Library Cataloguing in Publication Data
LeFanu, W. R.
A bibliography of Edward Jenner. – 2nd ed.
1. Jenner, Edward – Bibliography
I. Title    II. LeFanu, W. R. Bio-bibliography of
Edward Jenner, 1749–1823
016.6145'21        Z8452/

ISBN 0 906795 19 2

Typeset in Linotron 202 Bembo by
Rowland Phototypesetting Ltd,
Bury St Edmunds, Suffolk
Printed in Great Britain by
St Edmundsbury Press,
Bury St Edmunds, Suffolk

To the memory of
SIR GEOFFREY KEYNES
Surgeon      Scholar      Bibliographer
a friend for fifty years

# Preface

THE FIRST EDITION of this Bibliography was compiled in 1947 and 1948 when the bicentenary of Edward Jenner's birth in 1749 was coming near. As custodian of John Hunter's papers at the Royal College of Surgeons of England I became interested in the writings of the Hunterian school, prominent medical men whom Hunter had taught or influenced. It was surprising to find how little was known about Hunter's most famous pupil Edward Jenner, beyond his discovery of vaccination and the controversy in which it involved him. Everything seemed to be copied from the official biography published more than a century earlier, except for Dawtrey Drewitt's study of his work in natural history.

*An Inquiry into Cowpox*, Jenner's epoch-making book of 1798, was a classic often reprinted. The great innovators – Pasteur, Lister, Pirquet – had praised him as the inspirer of their work for immunization and preventive medicine. The other books and articles, which he published without intermission through the last twenty years of his life, had hardly been looked at since they first appeared, though the development of his thought and teaching can be traced only through them. As the relative rarity of copies of his writings was unknown, I circulated a check-list to libraries in the United Kingdom, Europe, North America and Australasia, which received a generous response. From this cooperation I printed lists of copies of each edition described in the Bibliography. This pioneer effort does not need to be repeated, now that the American copies are recorded in the *National Union Catalog of pre-1965 Imprints*. I have restricted my lists to inscribed copies showing Jenner's personal contacts, many of which, on both sides of the Atlantic, I have been privileged to examine; for a few rare publications I have recorded all copies known to me. Jenner was confident that vaccination could eradicate smallpox completely. One hundred and eighty years later the vaccination campaigns of the World Health Organization have proved him right; the achievement of the eradication of smallpox was announced on 8 May 1980.

In this second edition I have corrected errors and incorporated editions and articles which I had missed, though none of major importance. I have renumbered the entries in a single sequence, repeating the old number in square brackets when it had to be changed. I thank many friends – physicians and historians, librarians and booksellers – for generous communication of knowledge, in particular Gertrude Annan, Derrick Baxby, Renate Burgess, the late Hugh K. Elliott, Genevieve Miller, and Paul Saunders; special items are acknowledged in the text. I am deeply in debt to Eustace Cornelius and Ian Lyle at the Library of the Royal College of Surgeons of England for constant help, especially with the illustrations, also to Robert Cross, Alwyne Wheeler and David Way for their expert advice.

WILLIAM LeFANU

# Contents

# Illustrations

Permission to reproduce illustrations from books in their possession is gratefully acknowledged to The John Rylands University of Manchester Library (3); The National Library of Malta (59); New York Academy of Medicine (26, 114A); Royal College of Surgeons of England (MS 1, 23); Wellcome Institute Library, London (8, 116, 139).

# Abbreviations

The code-symbols used for libraries vary in all the standard union catalogues, some alphabetized under American States, others by city names, or arbitrarily; I use a simple series of the initials of the libraries, and those mentioned only a few times are named in full in the text. Locations are not given for periodicals, British and American union lists of holdings being available.

| | |
|---|---|
| BL | British Library Reference Division, London |
| BLO | Bodleian Library, Oxford |
| BmMI | Birmingham Medical Institute |
| BUL | Birmingham University Library |
| CLM | Countway Library of Medicine, Boston, incorporating Boston and Harvard Medical Libraries |
| EUL | Edinburgh University Library |
| LC | Library of Congress, Washington |
| LML | Lane Medical Library, Stanford University, Palo Alto, California |
| LSH | London School of Hygiene and Tropical Medicine |
| MiU | University of Michigan Library, Ann Arbor |
| MML | Manchester Medical Library, John Rylands University of Manchester Library |
| MSK | Medical Society of the County of Kings, Brooklyn, New York |
| NLM | National Library of Medicine, Bethesda, Maryland |
| NWU | Northwestern University Medical School Library, Chicago |
| NYAM | New York Academy of Medicine |
| OLM | Osler Library, McGill University, Montreal |
| PL | Public Library |
| RACP | Royal Australasian College of Physicians, Sydney |
| RACS | Royal Australasian College of Surgeons, Melbourne |
| RCP | Royal College of Physicians, London |

RCPE        Royal College of Physicians of Edinburgh

RCPI        Royal College of Physicians of Ireland

RCS         Royal College of Surgeons of England

RFPSG       Royal Faculty of Physicians and Surgeons of Glasgow

StBH        St Bartholomew's Hospital, London

UL          University Library

WHM         Wellcome Institute for the History of Medicine, London

WML(J)      Welch Medical Library (Jacobs collection), Baltimore, Maryland

ViU         University of Virginia Library, Charlottesville

YMH         Yale Medical Historical Library, New Haven, Connecticut

The following abbreviations are given for cited published works:

Baron       John Baron *The Life of Edward Jenner*, vols 1–2, 1827–38

Baxby       Derrick Baxby *Jenner's Smallpox Vaccine* 1981

Miller      Genevieve Miller, ed. *Letters of Edward Jenner from the Henry Barton Jacobs Collection in the William H. Welch Medical Library*, Baltimore 1983

Ottley      Drury Ottley 'The Life of John Hunter' in Hunter's *Works*, vol. 1, 1835

Saunders    Paul Saunders *Edward Jenner, the Cheltenham Years* 1982

# Edward Jenner:
# a biographical introduction

EDWARD JENNER was born at Berkeley in Gloucestershire on 17 May 1749. His life divides into three almost equal stages. Till the age of twenty-four he acquired a good education and a thorough medical training, while he developed his inborn tastes as a naturalist. Next, he practised as a country surgeon for twenty-five years from 1773 till he announced his discovery of vaccination in 1798 when he was forty-nine. From then till he died in his seventy-fourth year, 1823, he was deeply engaged in practice as a physician at Cheltenham and London as well as at Berkeley, and in his ever-widening campaign to eradicate smallpox from the world.

His forebears were minor gentry long settled around Berkeley, many of them clergymen. He was the youngest of a large family, lost his parents while a child, and grew up in the care of elder brothers and sisters, Stephen the eldest brother directing his education. Stephen was a Fellow of Magdalen College, Oxford, and succeeded their father as Vicar of Berkeley. From schools at Wotton-under-Edge and Cirencester, Edward was apprenticed to Abraham Ludlow, the country surgeon at Chipping Sodbury near Bristol, for his preliminary medical training. He entered St George's Hospital, London in October 1770 as John Hunter's first house pupil; Hunter was the rising star among London's surgeons. Jenner became his assistant in practice and research, and was deeply influenced by Hunter's insatiable search for knowledge at the bedside of the sick, in pathological dissection, and through experiments. Hunter was already forming his Museum of anatomy and pathology. Jenner learned from him to explore physiological function experimentally in the living animal and relate it to anatomical structure; he also learned the skill of preparing delicate specimens for display. In two years he was equipped to commence a potentially successful career in the capital; but he chose instead to practise at home in the country.

The first chapter of this Bibliography describes the variety of subjects on which Hunter encouraged him to work. Most of Jenner's results were recorded in reports included in Hunter's writings. One subject he made his own, the quasi-parasitic breeding habits of the cuckoo. His discovery that the young cuckoo itself ejects its foster-nestlings was too surprising to be readily accepted, but it won him the Fellowship of the Royal Society in 1789 and was acclaimed by French and Italian naturalists.

Jenner's remarkable insight, leaping ahead of apparent evidence, first showed itself in this animal research. Set by Hunter to study changes of temperature in hibernating animals, he realized that a physiological exchange was involved, and noticed the sequence of physiological rhythms. This he applied to the problems of bird migration: Jenner was the first to see that it is provoked by a seasonal sexual change. Though much remained to be elucidated, he directed this research onto the right path.

He did not neglect medical practice, however, and promoted clubs in his neighbourhood where he could discuss medical questions with his colleagues. The two most notable matters were angina pectoris and prevention of smallpox. William Heberden in London had described the paroxysmal thoracic oppression of angina in 1768–72, and twenty years later Jenner's close friend Caleb Parry of Bath established that functional inadequacy of the arteries is a main factor in this disease. Jenner meanwhile had shown by dissection that the structural cause was obstructive hardening of the coronary arteries.

The same instinctive ability to draw far-seeing conclusions from small observations lay behind Jenner's understanding that the various pox diseases of animals and man are caused by related 'viruses' or 'poisons' in their exudates. His explanation of this belief was rudimentary, since he had to rely on clinical experience without microscopic research. Nothing was known of microorganisms: bacteria had been forgotten, though seen by Leeuwenhoek a century earlier, while viruses in the modern sense were not differentiated till 1892. His intuition that a mild disease can ward off another more severe, though it proved correct, may have come to him from Hunter's erroneous teaching that two constitutional diseases cannot coexist in the same host.

During the 1790s, while trying inoculation of the pox diseases of horses, pigs, and cows, Jenner improved his professional standing. He received the degree of MD from St Andrews University, and began a summer practice at Cheltenham, the growing spa-town some twenty miles from Berkeley, which he continued till 1815. Little was known about his activity there before the publication of Paul Saunders's thorough history of his 'Cheltenham Years' in 1982. Saunders shows from his intimate knowledge of local records that Jenner became a leading citizen there, and engaged the influence of important residents and visitors in promoting his vaccination campaign.

My second chapter discusses the content of his epoch-making *Inquiry into the Variolae Vaccinae, the Cow Pox*, published in London in June 1798, with a survey of its later editions and translations into several languages. In this he advocated an entirely new procedure, inoculation of a mild non-contagious disease in prevention of another which was contagious and dangerous, even deadly. Moreover he proposed inoculating this preventive from person to person to create a protected population, a first step towards public hygiene and immunology.

Though this was quickly welcomed, some of Jenner's followers encountered difficulties in carrying out his procedure. Controversy arose and was met by Jenner, sometimes too impatiently, in a long series of pamphlets and contributions to the medical press. These publications are enumerated and discussed in the third chapter. The development of his thought and the withdrawal of some early claims, which led to unfair accusations of deceit, may be traced particularly through his papers *Varieties and Modifications of the Vaccine Pustule* (1804–06) and *Facts unobserved respecting Variolous Contagion* (1808).

I have dealt solely with Jenner's own publications, without describing the writings of his critics or supporters, except so far as seemed necessary to clarify the course of his work. The whole story is told, with explanatory evidence from recent virological research, in Derrick Baxby's book *Jenner's Smallpox Vaccine* (1981).

Jenner visited London for several months each year from 1798 to 1814, and practised there during 1801 to 1805, busily engaged vaccinating, answering his critics, and corresponding with supporters at home and abroad. He also promoted the work of the Royal Jennerian Society for the Extermination of the Smallpox from 1803 and of the National Vaccine Institution from 1808, though often irritated by faults he found in their administration.

He had married Catherine Kingscote, daughter of a Gloucestershire family, in 1788, but their private life was darkened by the mental handicap of their elder son, who died in 1810; Catherine's own health was also failing for some years before her death in 1815. After that time Jenner seldom left Berkeley, but he continued to work and in 1821 issued a *Circular Letter*, widely reproduced in journals and newspapers, to confirm his complete confidence in vaccination when performed with the strict attention to detail which he had always advocated.

The later chapters of the Bibliography describe his last publications, including the speculative *Letter to Charles Henry Parry* (1822), which reverted to the doctrine of 'sympathies' between different constitutional or diseased conditions, and the remarkably far-sighted and innovatory *Migration of Birds*, written probably in the 1790s but published posthumously by his nephew. A few other posthumous publications, a survey of his correspondence, and some account of biographies and memorabilia complete the story.

After a very short period of failing health Edward Jenner died at Berkeley, from a cerebral stroke, on 26 January 1823 – four months before his seventy-fourth birthday. He was survived by a son and a daughter.

# CHAPTER 1

# Experiments and Observations

'Il s'est trouvé des gens d'assez mauvais goût pour hasarder quelques plaisanteries sur le choix d'un pareil sujet. Je les renvoie au travail de Jenner et les invite à imiter cette sagacité, cette pénétration appliquées il est vrai à un petit objet, si tant est que pour un vrai savant il y ait de petits objets'.

> Paul-Joseph Lorain, 'Eloges – Jenner', in Faculté de Médecine de Paris, *Conférences historiques* . . . *1865* (1866), p. 339; the 'petit objet' was Jenner's study of cuckoos.

Education for a medical career in England in the eighteenth century was usually by apprenticeship to a local surgeon-apothecary. When a young man aspired to become a physician he went on to graduate from the medical faculty of a university – more often at Edinburgh, Dublin or Leiden than Oxford or Cambridge. The less ambitious spent a year or two working in the hospital of a large city.

When Edward Jenner, aged twenty-one, completed his apprenticeship under Abraham Ludlow, who practised at Chipping Sodbury near Bristol, he was accepted as a pupil by John Hunter in London. Jenner became Hunter's surgical dresser at St George's Hospital, and his assistant in private practice and anatomical research as his earliest house-pupil at Jermyn Street.

John Hunter was already well-known at forty-two for his anatomical work and was becoming recognized as a progressive surgeon. His influence on Jenner was profound and lasting. Jenner became eager, like Hunter, to seek the underlying causes of disease by dissection and by comparison of case histories, and did not neglect comparative anatomy. When Jenner went home to practise at Berkeley near Gloucester, Hunter set him to work on problems of natural history. 'There is imployment for you, young man' he wrote in the summer of 1773; 'I hear you saying, there is no end to your wants'. They lived more than a day's journey apart, yet collaborated in a wide range of biological research for twenty years, till Hunter died in October 1793.

Hunter included Jenner's reports in his published papers, but Jenner himself published little. In 1783–84 he wrote a pamphlet and an article on a new method of preparing emetic tartar – a medicine based on antimony, then much in vogue – and in 1788 the Royal Society published his observations on the breeding habits and anatomy of the cuckoo, a notable advance in knowledge of bird behaviour. Both these efforts had been promoted by Hunter. Jenner followed Hunter's example also when he formed societies in his neighbourhood for friendly discussion of medical problems.

## I  Banks's South Sea Specimens

In 1817 Jenner's friend James Moore, Director of the National Vaccine Institute in London, wrote in his book *The History and Practice of Vaccination* that while Jenner was John Hunter's pupil in 1771–72 'Hunter recommended him to aid Sir Joseph Banks in forming a scientific arrangement of the curiosities and productions, which he had brought from the islands in the South Sea . . . . When a second voyage of discovery was projected, Jenner was solicited to be one of the literary associates in that enterprise. This was declined, and the project was afterwards abandoned'. Banks and Jenner were still active in 1817 when this note was published; ten years later, after both had died, John Baron repeated Moore's statement, with slight embellishment, in his *Life of Edward Jenner* (1827).

The story was never contradicted, but there seems to be no evidence for it from 1771–72, forty-five years before Moore wrote. Much work has been done lately in surveying the records and surviving specimens from Banks's uncompleted project of arranging and publishing the collections from the *Endeavour* voyage (1768–71) and his abortive plan to lead a new scientific team on James Cook's second voyage, in the *Resolution* which sailed in 1772, but no record of participation by Jenner has been found. Hunter certainly knew Banks before 1768, but the first record of acquaintance between Banks and Jenner is an exchange of letters in 1787. (See VIII, below.)

Jenner did not intend to practise in London, nor wish to travel; he preferred to spend his life as a country surgeon in his native Gloucestershire. Hunter, who shared and shaped Jenner's interest in natural history, wrote to him regularly after he had gone home to Berkeley, asking for specimens and seeking his help in definite projects. According to John

6

Baron, his biographer, Jenner kept a manuscript record of his experiments, but it is not known to survive.

## II  HIBERNATION AND THE HEDGEHOG

When Hunter became interested in hypothermia and the limit to which animals tolerate external cold, he experimented by freezing live fish and the ears of rabbits and studying their recovery. He went on to explore the physiology of hibernating dormice and hedgehogs.

Hunter and Jenner did not use the term 'hibernation', which was loosely used since the late seventeenth century for winter seclusion; it became restricted early in the nineteenth century to the condition which Hunter called 'the sleeping season' or 'the torpid state', in contrast to 'the voluntary state', in certain small animals. Similarly they used the words 'common air' and 'atmosphere' loosely without differentiation, and printed their temperature readings without indicating the scale, though Hunter once wrote '109° Fahrenheit' (the Fahrenheit scale can be presumed). The word 'atmosphere' was currently used to mean 'the air in a particular place as affected by heat or cold', but at this time in 1783 Henry Cavendish was beginning experiments which led forty years later to definition of atmospheric pressure.

When Hunter could not readily find live hedgehogs near London he asked Jenner to send them from the West Country. 'Dear Jenner, I received yours by Dr. Hicks with the hedgehog alive; I put it into my garden, but I want more', he wrote about 1776, adding in a postscript 'I should suppose hedgehogs would come in a box, full of holes all round, filled with hay, and some fresh meat put into it'. Hunter saw that the crucial point to be determined was the mechanism of temperature maintenance; his work was the first useful contribution to this problem, which has been fully explored only in the present century. Hunter set Jenner to make experiments on the heat of hedgehogs, parallel to his own dormice experiments. It was about one of these that he wrote on 2 August 1775 'I thank you for your experiment on the hedgehog; but why do you ask me a question by the way of solving it? I think your solution is just; but why think, why not try the experiment? Repeat all the experiments upon a hedgehog as soon as you receive this, and they will give you the solution'. He set Jenner to compare the body-temperature of hibernating hedgehogs with their normal summer temperature.

Hunter's 'Experiments and observations on animals with respect to the power of producing heat' was published in his book *Observations on certain Parts of the Animal Oeconomy* (1786); this article was expanded from papers published by the Royal Society in 1778 and 1779. In the second of those he had said that he had not had opportunities of examining hedgehogs 'in their involuntary state'. In the expanded paper he wrote: 'As I was unable to procure hedgehogs in the torpid state . . . I got my friend Mr. Jenner, surgeon, at Berkeley, to make the same experiments on that animal, that I might compare them with those in the dormouse; and his account is as follows . . .'.

Jenner described three experiments on hibernating hedgehogs, one on an active hedgehog, and one on a puppy. 'In the winter', he reported 'the atmosphere at 44°, the heat of a torpid hedgehog in the pelvis was 45° . . . in summer the atmosphere 78°, the heat of the hedgehog, in an active state, in the cavity of the abdomen towards the pelvis was 95°, at the diaphragm 97°'.

Hunter mentioned hedgehogs again and again in his letters to Jenner. In December 1777 he wrote 'I put three hedgehogs in the garden but they all died . . . I want you to find out their haunts and observe what they do', adding after varied instructions 'in short, make what observations you can'; in March 1778 'I am hedgehogless'; in September, hearing of Jenner's disappointment in a love-affair, 'Let her go, never mind her. I shall employ you with hedgehogs'; in November 'I don't know if hedgehogs burrow'; 'How do hedgehogs go on?' he asked in January, and a little later proposed an experiment to see if they digest during torpor.

Hunter's 'Some observations on digestion' in his *Observations on the Animal Oeconomy* is almost entirely a new paper, though incorporating previous work which had been read to the Royal Society. In this paper he quoted an account by Jenner of an experiment on 'the hedgehog which was the subject of the third experiment' published in the paper on animal heat.

Jenner described how 'The hedgehog, while the heat of the stomach was at 30°, had neither desire for food, nor power of digesting it; but when increased by inflammation in the abdomen to 93°, the animal seized a toad which happened to be in the room, and upon being offered some bread and milk, it immediately ate it'. Jenner perhaps saw that an exchange was involved in the hibernating animal's reduction of body heat, but in effect he measured merely the amount of the loss. This research made him aware of physiological rhythms, which he studied further a few years later in relation to bird migration.

8

1    [Experiments on hedgehogs in 1779] in Hunter's *Observations on . . . the Animal Oeconomy* (1786) pp. 99–100; (1792) p. 112; *Works of John Hunter*, 4 (1835), 143.

2    [Experiments on digestion during hibernation (1779)] in Hunter's *Observations on . . . the Animal Oeconomy* (1786) p. 155; (1792) p. 195; *Works* (1835) vol. 4, p. 88.

## III   THE FREE MARTIN

Hunter's 'Account of the Free Martin' in which he described and discussed the occurrence of bisexual individuals in cattle was read to the Royal Society on 25 February 1779, and published in the *Philosophical Transactions*, 69 (1779), 279–93. Hunter did not mention Jenner in this paper, though he sent him a copy, but long afterwards Jenner wrote to his friend Richard Worthington on 5 April 1810 'I was the first who made the fact known some thirty years ago to Mr Hunter'. It had long been known to cattle breeders, and was noticed by Malpighi in 1692.

## IV   EMETIC TARTAR

Jenner's first pamphlet, without date or author's name, was printed by the bookseller at Wotton-under-Edge. He was dissatisfied with the preparations of some medicines in common use and made experiments, in particular to obtain a preparation of emetic tartar which would be 'regular in strength and uniform in operation'. The pamphlet was printed in the autumn of 1783, for Hunter acknowledged it in November 'I received your little publication with the Tart. Emet. I have a great deal to say about it . . . I approve of it much and will do all in my power to promote the sale . . . I would desire you to burn your book, for you will have all the world making it', and he wrote again to the same purpose a month or two later. Jenner preferred to make his work freely available. He continued to experiment and Hunter wrote to him in May 1784 'I wish you would draw out the process for making the tartar emetic. The physicians that I have given it to speak well of it as a more certain medicine than the other', and

EXPERIMENTS AND OBSERVATIONS

he suggested that Jenner should send an account of the process to his Society for the Improvement of Medical and Chirurgical Knowledge. Jenner accordingly described his method of obtaining pure emetic tartar crystals; this paper, with his letter of 5 February, was read to the Society on 4 June 1784 but not published until 1793. Jenner also experimented from about 1790 with the application of emetic tartar ointment as a counter-irritant, and published an account of his results in 1822. (Chapter 4, II.)

Tartar emetic (Antimony, Potassium tartrate) is recorded in *Martindale's Extra Pharmacopoeia* 27th ed. (1977) and in the [British] *Pharmaceutical Codex* 11th ed. (1979) for the treatment of the tropical helminth and protozoal infections such as schistosomiasis (bilharziasis) and leish-maniasis (kala-azar) with warning of its undesirable effects.


**3** Cursory Observations on Emetic Tartar; Wherein is pointed out an improved Method of preparing Essence of Antimony, by a Solution of Emetic Tartar in Wine [*rule*] Wotton-under-Edge. Printed by J. Bence, Bookseller and Stationer.

COLLATION: 8°: A⁶:11 pp.:188 mm.

CONTENTS: A1ᵃ Title; A1ᵇ blank; A2ᵃ–A4ᵇ, pp. (3)–8 Text; [*ornament*] Cursory Observations on Emetic Tartar, etc. Since that important Aera. . . .; A5ᵃ–6ᵃ, pp. 9–11: [*double rule*] Essence of Antimony is commonly made. . . .; A6ᵇ blank.

COPIES: BL, MML, NLM. (Printed anonymously, but the recorded copies are signed by Jenner, and have MS corrections in his hand.)

NOTE: Jenner stated at pp. 6–7: 'In this Preparation, the Reguline part of the Antimony is fully saturated with the Cream of Tartar . . . it may be kept rubbed down with double refined Sugar', and at pp. 10–11: 'a very elegant Antimonial Essence or Wine, in which the dose may be ascertained with the utmost precision may be extemporaneously prepared, by dissolving sixty-four Grains of the Emetic Tartar [*added in MS*: previously reduced to an impalpable powder] in a Pint of Madeira, Mountain, or any good White Wine. In this Solution, allowing sixty Drops to a Drachm, fifteen Drops will contain an eighth part of a grain of Emetic Tartar'.


**4** A process for preparing pure Emetic Tartar by Re-crystallization. By Mr. Jenner, Surgeon at Berkeley. In a letter to John Hunter, Esq. Read June 4, 1784. *Transactions of a Society for the Improvement of Medical and Chirurgical Knowledge*, London, 1 (1793), 30–33.

# *C U R S O R Y*

# OBSERVATIONS

### O N

# EMETIC TARTAR;

Wherein is pointed out an improved Method
of preparing

## ESSENCE OF ANTIMONY,

### B Y  A  S O L U T I O N

### O F

# EMETIC TARTAR

### I N  W I N E.

---

WOTTON-UNDER-EDGE:
Printed by J. BENCE, Bookseller and Stationer;

[ 1783.]

Emetic Tartar (1783)

CONTENTS: Pp. 30–31 Letter, signed Edward Jenner, Berkeley, February 5, 1784; pp. 32–33 The Process for preparing pure Emetic Tartar by Re-crystallization.

COPY USED: RCS.

NOTE: Jenner stated, pp. 30–31: 'the practitioner, wanting a fixt criterion of its quality, must often prescribe with uncertainty, and generally be disappointed in his conclusions . . . emetic tartar made according to the inclosed process will bear the test of a scrupulous examination. It will be found to be a pure neutral salt composed entirely of tartar and the reguline part of antimony, formed in crystals beautifully white and transparent, and perfectly soluble either in water or wine . . .'. The process consisted in a series of repeated boilings and crystallizations of a mixture of cream of tartar and glass of antimony.

5    A German translation of the *Transactions* was published in 1797: *Abhandlungen der Londonschen Gesellschaft zur Vermehrung der medizinischen und chirurgischen Wissenschaften*. Aus dem englischen mit Anmerkungen von Theod. Geo. Aug. Roose. Braunschweig bei Chr. Friedr. Thomas; Leipzig, bei Schmidt, Nauck 1797. (Recorded by A. C. P. Callisen, *Medicinisches Schriftsteller-Lexicon*, 25 (1837), 806 b).

## V  OPHTHALMIA

In 1783 Jenner recommended the use of a seton in the temple when emetic tartar ointment failed to cure a severe ophthalmia. In a letter to Richard Worthington on 25 September 1809 he wrote of the ointment: 'Practice says spare it not when the eye itself is as red as a cherry . . . In cases of the most violent kind, and which quickly threaten to destroy the eye, I introduce a seton in the temple, about an inch from the outward angle of the eye . . . The latter practice has, I really believe, given sight to thousands since I first made it public about the year 1783'. No separate publication of this proposal appears to have survived.

Hunter asked him on 26 January 1784 for his paper on the ophthalmia for the Society for the Improvement of Medical and Chirurgical Knowledge; in a letter of about 1786 he wrote 'I have long been expecting a long letter from you informing me of your method of curing ophthalmias'. Baron had seen a manuscript *Treatise on ophthalmia* which Jenner had read to the Gloucestershire Medical Society; he described it as systematic, bearing marks of close and accurate discrimination of the symptoms and varieties of the disease. To the modern ophthalmologist the seton seems a blunderbuss intervention.


## VI  THE BOTTLENOSED WHALE

On 28 June 1787 Hunter presented to the Royal Society his largest and most memorable zoological paper *Observations on the Structure and Oeconomy of Whales*. It was published in the *Philosophical Transactions*, 77 (1787), 371–450 with plates XVI–XXIII.

In the list of whales which he had dissected Hunter recorded that 'Of the Delphinus Delphis, or Bottle-nose Whale (Tab. XVIII) I had one sent to me by Mr Jenner, Surgeon, at Berkeley. It was about eleven feet long . . .'. Jenner's whale was the Bottlenosed Dolphin *Tursiops truncatus*, confused by Hunter with the Common Dolphin *Delphinus delphis*. The explanation of plate XVIII gives the following detail: 'Fig. 1. A species of Bottle-nose Whale; the Delphinus Delphis of Linnaeus. It was caught upon the sea-coast, near Berkeley, where it had been for several days, following its mother, and was taken along with the old one, and sent up to me whole, for examination, by Mr Jenner, Surgeon, at Berkeley. The old one was eleven feet long. Fig. 2. The head of the same whale as fig. 1. to shew the shape of the blow-hole . . . '. Hunter refers incidentally at p. 383 to 'The small Bottle-nose Whale, caught near Berkeley', and at p. 446 he gave the opinion that 'The milk [of whales] is probably very rich; for in that caught near Berkeley with its young one, the milk which was tasted by Mr Jenner and Mr Ludlow, surgeon at Sodbury, was rich like Cow's milk to which cream had been added'.

Hunter's letters of 12 and 16 April 1776 gave precise directions for sending the whales: 'The large porpoise I would have coarsely stripped and the bones put into a cask and sent; the young one if not too large put into spirits to be able to inject it . . . It came quite fresh and is under dissection and drawing, . . . was the milk sweet? Could you save some of it, if but two drops to see if it grows sour'.

## VII  THE JACKAL

In the opening paragraphs of *An Inquiry into Cow Pox* Jenner, writing of the domestication of animals, said 'the late Mr. John Hunter proved, by experiments, that the dog is the wolf in a degenerate state'. Hunter's 'Observations tending to show that the Wolf, Jackal, and Dog, are all of the same species' was published in the *Philosophical Transactions* (1787) with 'A supplementary Letter' in 1789. When Hunter revised these papers for the enlarged edition of *Observations on the Animal Oeconomy* (1792) he added new observations showing that half-breed animals and those that are three removes from a wild ancestor have 'a propensity to fall back into their original instinctive principles'. To illustrate this assertion he prints an 'account from Mr. Jenner of Berkeley to whom I gave a second remove jackal, viz. three parts dog': 'The little jackal-bitch which you gave me is grown a fine handsome animal; but she certainly does not possess the understanding of common dogs. She is easily lost when I take her out, and is quite inattentive to a whistle. She is more shy than a dog, and starts frequently when a quick motion is made before her. Of her inches she is uncommonly fleet, much more so than any dog I ever saw. She can turn a rabbit in the field; she is fond of stealing away and lying about the adjacent meadows, where her favourite amusement is hunting the field mouse, which she catches in a particular manner'.

6      ['Account of a half-breed jackal'] in Hunter's *Observations on . . . the Animal Oeconomy*, second edition (1792), p. 156; *Works*, 4 (1835), 329–30.

## VIII  FOX AND DOG

Hunter in his first paper on the wolf, jackal and dog, mentioned above, which he read to the Royal Society on 26 April 1787, gave his opinion that the fox was of the same genus as the dog, adding 'it is confidently asserted by many that the fox breeds with the dog but this has not been accurately ascertained, . . . and once breeding does not constitute a species'. Jenner was in London during this spring, when Joseph Banks, P.R.S. since 1778, appears to have raised this question with him; after he had gone home he wrote to Banks in June sending a report from an unnamed acquaintance, who describes unsuccessful mating of a dog-fox with a terrier bitch:

'notwithstanding the above' Jenner added 'almost every sportsman asserts that foxes and dogs will produce an offspring. But I shall use every endeavour to set the matters clear, by experiments with these animals'.

## IX  ANIMAL MANURES

In the same letter Jenner reported to Banks a series of experiments which he had made in 1780, 1781 and 1782. 'I wish they were more worthy your observation' he wrote, 'though they do not go far enough to determine whether animal manure will produce lasting good effects on vegetables, they prove that a superabundance of this substance is destructive to vegetable life. I shall copy these notes as they stand in my journal'.

The manures used were (1) the serum of human blood on grass, and on mustard seed; (2) the coagulated part of the blood mixed with the serum on mustard seed; (3) equal parts of serum and water on the same; (4) blood mixed with wood ashes and powdered chalk on polyanthus plants. The first and fourth were found to produce rapid and vigorous growth, but the polyanthus soon withered.

In a second series of experiments on peaches and currants Jenner used (1) the coagulated part of fresh blood; (2) equal parts of blood and common mould; (3) common garden mould, from time to time moistened with the serum of blood; (4) a control or 'standard' in common mould. Only those treated at no. (4) were consistently healthy, though those at no. (3) recovered from a sickly condition.

## X  THE CUCKOO

Soon after Jenner had settled at Berkeley he must have offered to make observations for Hunter. In one of the earliest letters of their correspondence Hunter wrote 'I am obliged to you for thinking of me, especially in my natural history. I shall be glad of your observations on the cuckoo and upon the breeding of toads: be as particular as you can'. Hunter thanked him for stomachs of cuckoos when he was investigating the hairballs which Jenner reported 'I should like to have a few more . . . If possible I wish you could remove the cuckoo's egg into another bird's nest and tame the young one to see what note it has. There is imployment for you, young man! . . . Do you keep an account of the observations on the cuckoo, or must I refer to your letters? I want a nest with the eggs in it: also one with a young cuckoo; also an old cuckoo'. In April 1776, when busy with the bottlenosed whale, he added 'Did I write to you some time ago about cuckoos? I have forgot; if I did not I must give you a long order'.

In May 1784, when writing about emetic tartar and about another porpoise, he reverted to the subject: 'I want the cuckoo cleared up: I am afraid it is now too late. I wish you would shoot an old one for me and send its gizzard in spirits', and in two letters of 1785 'I request the whole history of the cuckoo this summer from you' and 'you must pursue the cuckoo this summer'. A year later he asks for 'a long letter with the history of cuckoos'. In the winter of 1786–87 Jenner at last drafted an account of his observations for which Hunter thanked him 'and what further observations you can make I shall be glad to have them, or even a repetition of the former will be very acceptable'.

On 29 March 1787 Hunter presented Jenner's paper at the Royal Society, which possesses Jenner's holograph of this draft. It is written on thirty separate leaves of quarto paper; leaf 6 is omitted from the foliation; an unnumbered leaf, which ought to be at the front, has been bound between leaves 7 and 8: this is inscribed in another hand 'XXIII *Observations on the Natural History of the Cuckoo* by Mr. [Edward? in pencil] Jenner; In a letter to John Hunter Esq., F.R.S. Read March 29, 1787. [In pencil:] To be revised by Mr. Hunter'. The MS is dated at the beginning in Jenner's hand: 'Berkley Feb. 20th, 1787'.

Much of this draft was used verbatim in the published paper, much had to be redrafted because here Jenner expressed the opinion that it is the foster-parent which ejects its own fledglings.

Leaves 29 and 30, conjoined, are written on both sides, whereas the others are written on the rectos only; they contain a short essay 'On the emigration of Birds' which is the germ of the Migration paper of 1824; this short essay has not been published.

The MS is signed (leaf 30b) 'E Jenner' and endorsed 'Jenner, Cuckoo. Cancelled at the desire of the author. C.B.' [Charles Blagden, Secretary of the Royal Society].

It is clear that this paper was accepted for publication and had been numbered by the editor for inclusion in the volume of *Philosophical Transactions* for 1787. Jenner was in London in the spring of this year, but there is no evidence for the story that he was asked by Banks to withdraw his paper till he had made further researches. During the summer he continued watching cuckoos, but his journal for this period, now at the

Royal College of Physicians, does not record his discovery on 18 June 1787 that it is the young cuckoo, not its foster-parent, which ejects the eggs and nestlings.

Banks's letter of 7 July 1787 was written after Jenner had told him of this discovery and asked his leave to withdraw the first paper. Banks told him 'the Council give you a full scope for altering it as you shall chuse. Another year we shall be glad to print it'. Jenner rewrote his paper to include a report of this discovery, finishing it on 27 December 1787. He sent it by Hunter to the Royal Society, and it was read there on 13 March 1788. In May 1788 Hunter wrote to tell Jenner that the offprint of the paper was ready: 'I have ordered 50 copies, 25 for you and 25 for myself to give to friends'. Jenner's paper aroused interest on the Continent and was translated into French and Italian.

## Summary of Jenner's Paper

The cuckoo arrives in Gloucestershire about 17 April. The female appears to mate with many males, lays its eggs in many nests and 'in common with all birds of passage' may continue to lay for several weeks after its arrival. Jenner observed eggs in the nests of hedge-sparrow, water-wagtail, titlark [meadow-pipit], yellow hammer, linnet, and whinchat; his particular observations were made on cuckoos reared by the hedge-sparrow. Cuckoos' eggs had never been observed damaged or rejected; the small birds brood for the ordinary length of time; when the young cuckoo hatches, the other young birds and any remaining eggs are thrown out. The foregoing facts were well known, but the causes had not been correctly observed.

OBSERVATION 1: Cuckoos' eggs in titlark's nest. OBSERVATION 2: Wagtail's nest: all the young birds except the cuckoo and one unhatched egg were thrown out; this egg was found to contain a mature chick ready to hatch. OBSERVATION 3: Hedge-sparrow's nest: Jenner observed the displacement of eggs on 20 June 1786, but was unable to believe the young cuckoo capable of it.

18 June 1787: Hedge-sparrow's nest: a detailed description of the method used by the young cuckoo to displace the other young birds and eggs, with an anatomical description of the back-mechanism of the young cuckoo.

9–13 July 1787:    A young cuckoo was rendered unable to displace and put into a hedge-sparrow's nest.

Jenner noticed that the cuckoo's egg is as small as the hedge-sparrow's; it varies in colour corresponding to the host's eggs. He pointed out its heavier weight, an observation, he wrote, not made by anyone else.

He suggested that the cuckoo lays in the nests of small birds because larger birds, which do not readily brood a second time, could not tolerate the destruction of so many young. He noted the 'menacing air' of the young cuckoo, and its voice like a young hawk's. He suggested that its victims make easy food for young mammals and reptiles.

27 June 1787: he noticed two cuckoos' eggs in one nest; in due course the stronger young cuckoo ejected the other after a struggle.

Why does the cuckoo neither build nor brood? The ancient authorities made no observations; modern authors had made unsubstantiated statements about the size and weight of the cuckoo's stomach being such that it would crush its own eggs. This was not true of the more heavily built owls. During the summer of 1786 Jenner observed a young cuckoo hatch a hedge-sparrow's egg which was laid after the cuckoo had developed beyond the ejecting stage. He therefore introduced eggs of a wagtail to another young cuckoo and was satisfied by the evidence of two trustworthy witnesses that they were successfully hatched.

What is the cause of the cuckoo's behaviour? Jenner believed it was the shortness of its period of passage and the great number of its progeny; the adult birds are in England only from mid-April till the first week of July. He compared the cuckoo with the domestic hen: in particular the anatomy of the ovaries and oviduct. As to its choice of small birds, he noticed the frequent remaking of nests by blackbird and robin; and the faculty of accelerating or retarding egg production in small birds. Jenner's dissections of the genital organs of male and female cuckoos were bought, after Hunter's death, for the Hunterian Museum at the Royal College of Surgeons.

The young cuckoo is sometimes provided with animal food by wagtails; sometimes with vegetable by hedge-sparrows, which usually provide wholly animal; linnets provide wholly vegetable; titlarks provide chiefly grass-hoppers. Many young cuckoos have remarkable hairballs, apparently from the horsehairs used in lining nests, some cuckoos have hairballs made entirely from hairs of hairy caterpillars.

The departure of the young cuckoos is successive during August. Up to this time they are still being fed or partly fed by their foster-parents, as young crows are still fed while beginning to feed themselves.

'The purpose of nature' is fulfilled by the actions both of the adult cuckoos, who could not hatch the large number of eggs which they lay, and of the young, because the little birds who hatch them could not provide enough food for their own brood and for the young cuckoo.

Jenner's careful descriptions have been confirmed by photography. F. Howard Lancum showed to the Linnean Society of London in 1929 a series of lantern slides reproducing the first photographs which clearly illustrate the various stages of the eviction process; the hollow in the back of the young cuckoo was demonstrated in preparations made by R. H. Burne FRS, physiological curator of the Hunterian Museum at the time. Jenner's most acute observation was that the cuckoo's egg can be distinguished by its weight when resembling the host's in size and colour. Julian Huxley (1927) recorded the disparate proportion of egg-weight to body-weight in the cuckoo, less than one third of the average among birds in general, in his study of the subject. It has been suggested by Ian Wyllie (1981) that the evolution of resemblance between the cuckoo's and the fosterer's eggs might have arisen from the constant return of one line of cuckoos to the same species of foster parent, if that could be proved. Teleological explanations may appear naive, but they are in keeping with Hunter's vitalist philosophy and the religious orthodoxy of the period. He promised in this paper to make further contributions about cuckoos and about the migration of birds.

Jenner was elected a Fellow of the Royal Society on 25 February 1789. His Fellowship was a formal recognition, now that he had submitted a paper to the Society, of the scientific ability long known to Banks and Hunter.

In the next generation Jenner's observations were dismissed by Charles Waterton, the eccentric traveller and naturalist. Norman Moore, who wrote the memoir of Jenner in the *Dictionary of National Biography* (1892), had edited in 1870 Waterton's *Natural History Essays*, which include the attack on Jenner's good faith, and later wrote in his memoir of Jenner that Waterton had demonstrated the absurdity of Jenner's account. Jenner's observations were accepted by the best ornithologists such as Alfred Newton, himself a friend of Moore; Charles Montagu had accepted them in 1802, and they were adopted in the posthumous (1812) edition of Thomas Pennant's *British Zoology*, the standard text of the time. Antivaccinists used Moore's mistake to argue that Jenner, wrong about the cuckoo, was wrong about vaccination: J. H. Levy's *The Bird that laid the Vaccination Egg* was published, like Moore's memoir, in 1892.

In our own time the value of Jenner's discoveries has been assessed by

Lawrence Kilham (1973) in considerable detail; he concluded that 'Jenner deserves recognition for having written the first comprehensive papers on two problems that are far from settled today, brood parasitism and migration, but also in providing a model of how field investigations in bird behaviour may be carried out'.

**7** 'Observations on the Natural History of the Cuckoo', *Philosophical Transactions*, 78, part 2 (1788), 219–37.

COLLATION: 2H¹a–2K²a

CONTENTS: P. 219: [*ornament*] Philosophical Transactions. [*rule*] XIV. Observations on the Natural History of the Cuckoo. By Mr. Edward Jenner. In a Letter to John Hunter, Esq., F.R.S. Read March 13, 1788. To John Hunter, Esq. Dear Sir, Having, at your request, employed some of my leisure hours in attending to the natural history of the Cuckoo . . . ; p. 237 ends: Edw. Jenner. Berkeley, December 27, 1787.

**8** [*rule*] Observations on the Natural History of the Cuckoo. From the Philosophical Transactions [*rule*].

COLLATION: 4°:χ1, A–B⁴, C²: 1 l, 19 pp.; 278 mm. [Not dated; issued May 1788].

CONTENTS: χ1ᵃ Title; A1ᵃ–C2ᵃ, pp. 3–19, Text: [*ornament*] Observations, etc. Read at the Royal Society, March 13, 1788. [*rule*] To John Hunter, Esq. Dear Sir, Having . . . ; C2ᵃ, p. 19, text ends . . . Edw. Jenner, Berkeley, December 27, 1787 [*ornament*].

COPIES USED: WHM, inscribed on title-page: 'From his friend the Author'; ViU, title-page inscribed 'W.D. 1788' (William Davies, brother-in-law of Jenner).

NOTE: This is the 'reprint' mentioned by Hunter in his letter of May 1788 to Jenner.

**9a** Observations on the Natural History of the Cuckoo from the Philosophical Transactions, *Literary Magazine and British Review* (March 1789), 179–87, omitting first and last paragraphs and n. 1 from p. 220 of original. (D. Baxby, in *Journal of the History of Medicine*, 36 (1981), 218–19.)

*From his friend the Author*

# O B S E R V A T I O N S

### ON THE

## NATURAL HISTORY

### OF THE

# C U C K O O.

From the PHILOSOPHICAL TRANSACTIONS.

The Cuckoo (1788)

**9b**    The Natural History of the Cuckoo, *The New Annual Register* . . .
*for the year 1788*, 9 (1789), 122–31, complete text omitting all footnotes.
(Information and photocopy given to me by Dr Derrick Baxby, 1983).

**10[9]**    Observations sur l'histoire naturelle du coucou Par M. Edward
Jenner: Extraits des Transactions Philosophiques, traduits par M.A.B.
. . . *Observations sur la physique, sur l'histoire naturelle et sur les arts*, Paris, 38
(1791), 161–71.

**11[10]**    Osservazioni sulla Storia Naturale del Cuculo, *Opusculi Scelti
sulle Scienze e sulle Arti tratti dagli Atti delle Accademie, e dalle altre Collezioni
Filosofiche e Letterarie, dalle Opere piu recenti Inglese, Tedesche, Francese,
Latine, e Italiane, e da Manoscritti originali e inediti*, Milano, 14 (1791),
154–64.

COPY USED: BL (Sir Joseph Banks's copy).

**12**    Osservazioni sull' Istoria naturale del Cucco [Abstract], *Giornale
per servire alla Storia ragionata della Medicina di questo Secolo*, Venice, 7
(1791), 547.

### XI  MEDICAL RESEARCHES: HEART DISEASE, SMALLPOX, ETC.

Jenner took a friendly part in several gatherings of medical men. The most
notable of these was the 'little society' instituted in May 1788, which met
three times a year for several years at The Fleece Inn at Rodborough near
Stroud in the north of Gloucestershire. Its formal name was the Gloucestershire Medical Society, but Jenner named it the Medico-convivial,
distinguishing it from the Convivio-medical which he frequented at The
Ship at Alveston in the south of the county. The meetings were on
Wednesdays.

The Fleece Society consisted of 'old friends, schoolfellows and fellow
students', the other original members being Caleb Hillier Parry of Bath,
Daniel Ludlow of Sodbury, son of Jenner's old master, John Heathfield
Hickes of Bristol, and Thomas Paytherus of Ross; Parry, Paytherus and

Jenner all addressed the society at various times on diseases of the heart; Jenner was President in 1790.

The society's papers came into the hands of Dr Alfred Henry Carter of Birmingham, who allowed an account of them to be published in 1896 at the centenary of Jenner's first vaccination: 'Records of an Old Medical Society: some unpublished manuscripts of Edward Jenner', *British Medical Journal*, 1 (1896), 1296–98.

This unsigned article includes the text of the following autographs of Jenner which are among the papers:

**13[11]**    'Remarks on the effects produced on the vessels about the head by mechanical obstructions to the passage of the blood through the cavities of the heart' (30 July 1788).

**14[12]**    'Report of a case of hydatids of the kidney, successfully treated with oil of turpentine' (28 July 1790). Jenner's work on hydatids is discussed in Chapter 5, section IV.

**15[13]**    'A fragment on swine pox inoculation' (September 1790). J. H. Hickes's report, 28 July 1790, on his and Jenner's work on swine-pox had mentioned that Jenner's one-year-old son had been inoculated with swine-pox on 17 December 1789 and with smallpox on 12 January 1790.

Jenner made other communications to the Society which are known only from their titles recorded in the minute-book:

**16[14]**    'Remarks on a disease of the heart following acute rheumatism, illustrated by dissections' (29 July 1789).

**17[15]**    'On the effects of calomel in relieving suppression of urine' (9 September 1789).

**18[16(a)]**     'A few particulars respecting a boy that passed an extraneous substance into the bladder, and another case of the sudden absorption of the fluid from an hydrocele' (Wednesday 13 June [1792] – not July as printed in 1896).

**19[16(b)]**     'An account of an extraneous body being introduced into the bladder of a boy 14 years of age' (25 July 1792).

The 'Regulations' of the Society are signed by the five original members.

Dr Carter sold these papers in October 1914 to Sir William Osler. They are described in *Bibliotheca Osleriana*, nos. 1267 and 1268, and were bequeathed by Osler to the Royal College of Physicians, London, except the 'Report of a case of hydatids of the kidney . . .' (no. 14) retained in the Osler Library at Montreal. The College received the papers on 4 October 1928; they form a volume of 69 leaves, 33 × 15·5 cm.

Jenner's lost paper on rheumatism of the heart (no. 16) seems to have anticipated the observations of the various authors quoted by W. C. Wells in his pioneer paper 'On rheumatism of the heart' which was read to the Society for the Improvement of Medical and Chirurgical Knowledge on 3 April 1810, and published in its *Transactions* 3 (1812), 373–424. On 10 January 1805 Jenner asked Parry to send him back his papers.

The problem of the cause of angina pectoris was at this time attracting attention. William Heberden the elder read to the Royal College of Physicians on 21 July 1768 a clinical description of 'a disorder of the breast' which he named 'angina pectoris'; this was published in the College's *Medical Transactions* (1772). A sufferer from the disease read a summary of the paper and wrote to Heberden offering his body for dissection. He died suddenly in the following autumn, when Heberden called in John Hunter to perform the autopsy. Jenner was present at this dissection; it was, he wrote in 1799 (**20**), 'the first case I ever saw of angina pectoris'. Heberden read the patient's letter and his own account of the dissection to the College on 17 November 1772, but it was not published till 1785.

Five years later Hunter was seized with the first attack of his illness, 'a swimming in the head' as he wrote to Jenner on 11 May 1777. He went to Bath from August to November 1777; Jenner visited him and recognized the signs of angina pectoris. In 1778 or 1785 Jenner and Paytherus examined the heart of a man who had died of angina. He now wrote to

Heberden to tell him that he thought Hunter was affected with many symptoms of angina pectoris.

This sequence of dates follows from Baron's dating of the letter to Heberden as 1778. He printed it from a draft found among Jenner's papers, and believed that it was never sent; Ottley says that it was communicated to Heberden. It seems possible that the letter ought to be dated 1786, following Hunter's second visit to Bath in the late summer of 1785 when the symptoms of his illness are known to have been more clearly defined. This later date would fit more reasonably with Heberden's publication of the 1772 case in 1785, and with the communications made to the Fleece Society by Jenner himself on mitral stenosis in July 1788, by Parry on angina pectoris in 1788 and by Paytherus 'on the dissection of a man who died of angina pectoris' in September 1789. Parry was a student at Edinburgh in 1777, but practising at Bath in 1785.

In the letter to Heberden, after mentioning Hunter's illness, Jenner wrote that among 'many victims of this dreadful disease' whom he had seen, he had 'only had two opportunities of an examination after death. In the first I found no material disease of the heart, except that the coronary artery appeared thickened . . . About three weeks ago Mr. Paytherus desired me to examine with him the heart of a person who had died of the Angina Pectoris a few days before. Here we found the same appearance of the coronary arteries . . . but what I had taken to be an ossification of the vessel itself, Mr. P. discovered to be a kind of firm fleshy tube within the vessel, with a considerable quantity of ossific matter dispersed irregularly through it . . . Is it possible this appearance may have been overlooked? How much the heart must suffer from [the coronary arteries] not being able to perform their functions (we cannot be surprised at the painful spasms) is a subject I need not enlarge upon, therefore I shall only remark that it is possible that all the symptoms may arise from this one circumstance'. Jenner says he hesitates to inform Hunter of his conclusions: 'I am fearful if Mr. H. should admit this, that it may deprive him of the hopes of a recovery'.

After Hunter's sudden death Everard Home wrote to Jenner on 18 February 1794 'It is singular that the circumstance you mentioned to me, and was always afraid to touch upon with Mr. Hunter, should have been a particular part of his own complaints, as the coronary arteries of the heart were considerably ossified'. Home described the post-mortem findings in his *Memoir* of Hunter and added 'It is reasonable to attribute the principal symptoms of the disease to an organic affection of the heart. That organ was rendered unable to carry on its functions'.

Parry's address of 1788 to the Fleece Society on angina pectoris was expanded into his book of 1799 *An Inquiry into the Symptoms and Causes of the Syncope anginosa, commonly called Angina Pectoris; illustrated by Dissections*, By Caleb Hillier Parry, MD . . . Bath, R. Cruttell; Cadell and Davies, London (1799).

Parry wrote here that the substance of his 'essay' was originally read to a Medical Society in Gloucestershire: 'In that Society the influence of the heart on the animal oeconomy had often been the subject of discussion . . . . It was suggested by Dr. Jenner, that the Angina Pectoris arose from some morbid change in the structure of the heart, probably ossification.' Many of Jenner's observations were communicated to the Society, and Parry himself had relied on the sagacity of Jenner in his diagnosis in the case of Mr. S. in 1788 described earlier in the book. He printed also Jenner's letter answering 'questions lately put to that excellent pathologist'. Jenner's 'letter' mentioned, first, Heberden's case in 1772, 'the first I ever saw, . . . the coronary arteries were not examined'; second, the case of Mr Carter at Dursley: when examining the heart, Jenner's 'knife struck against something so hard and gritty that I well remember looking up to the ceiling, conceiving that some plaster had fallen down'; third, the case examined with Paytherus: before beginning the dissection Jenner 'offered a wager' that they would find the coronary arteries ossified, 'this proved not to be exactly true, but a sort of cartilaginous canal was formed within the cavity of each artery'. Jenner and Paytherus 'concluded that malorganisation of these vessels was the cause of the disease'; fourth, he recalled Hunter's illness and that he had told his fears to Cline and Home, who had informed him of the post-mortem findings; fifth, Mr Bellamy's case.

Sir Thomas Lewis, the eminent London cardiologist, apportioned the credit due to Jenner and to Parry for this work, writing (1940) 'From the letter to Heberden it may be inferred that Jenner believed these coronary vessels to be unable to perform their functions . . . But he never committed himself to the view that angina pectoris is the outcome of functional imperfection . . . he emphasized the structural changes . . . Parry first grasped the significance of Jenner's observation and realized that functional efficiency rather than structural integrity of the arteries is of prime importance'. Thirty-five years later Dr Brian Livesley (1975) resolved the apparent contrast between Heberden's 'angina pectoris' and Parry's 'syncope anginosa'. Livesley concluded from Heberden's clinical description that his patients had severe obstructive coronary arterial disease with myocardial ischaemia, angina pectoris being precipitated by tachycardia induced by exertion, while Parry's patients had symptoms induced by bradycardia occurring at rest. Parry as a 'pathophysiologist' considered angina pectoris 'a mere case of syncope or fainting preceded by an unusual degree of anxiety or pain in the region of the heart'. From Jenner's observations Parry concluded that 'induration of the coronary arteries diminishes the energy of the heart, its readiness and degree of irritability'. Later physicians accepted Heberden's account and dismissed Parry's. From 'personal observations using radiotelemetric electrocardiography and atrial-pacing coronary sinus lactate studies' Livesley showed that Heberden and Parry described 'conditions at the opposite ends of the clinical spectrum of ischaemic heart disease'. He concluded from John Hunter's description of his own symptoms, which Jenner rightly interpreted as caused by ossification of the coronary arteries, that Hunter had suffered 'both the angina pectoris of Heberden and the syncope anginosa of Parry'.

**20[17]**    Letter to Caleb Hillier Parry on Angina Pectoris, in Parry, *An Inquiry into the Syncope Anginosa* (1799) pp. 3–5.

**21[18]**    Recherches sur les Symptomes et les Causes de la Syncope angineuse vulgairement appelée Angine de la Poitrine éclairées par les Ouvertures cadavériques par Caleb Hillier Parry . . . mises en français par A. Matthey . . . Paris, Patrix et Gilbert 1806. 8°: x, 116 pp; at pp. 4–7 Jenner's letter in French.

**22[19]**    Jenner's letter in German at pp. 44–45 of Erich Ebstein, *Aerzte-Briefe aus vier Jahrhunderten*, Berlin 1920.

# CHAPTER 2
# *The Cowpox Inquiry*

'The end of the eighteenth century was marked by a crucial epoch-making adventure in experimental medicine which was a prophetic prelude to the triumphs of the nineteenth and twentieth centuries, and which even today stands out as an unprecedented achievement in preventive medicine – Edward Jenner's successful cross-immunization experiments with cowpox'.

> Sir Lionel Whitby, President's Address to the British Medical Association (1948).

In June 1798 Edward Jenner announced his conviction that inoculation of cowpox, a mild non-contagious disease, was a tested protection against the dangerous contagious smallpox. He advocated the adoption of his method, soon called vaccination, as a routine procedure to replace variolation, inoculation of the exudate from smallpox lesions, the customary preventive for the previous seventy years. Jenner had undergone variolation with its debilitating regimen of blood-letting and starvation; he knew it was dangerous for the individual, often bringing on a severe attack of smallpox, and – by maintaining a pool of carriers – a source of epidemics.

He published the account of his experiments and method at his own expense in London as a slim quarto book, illustrated with coloured engravings of the mild pustules produced by cowpox infection. His book, modestly entitled *An Inquiry into the Causes and Effects of Variolae vaccinae, a Disease known by the name of the Cow-Pox*, caused a revolution in medical thought and practice. The title did not disclose the effects which the book claimed, but Jenner's invented 'Linnaean' binomial *Variola vaccina* 'cow smallpox', hints at his purpose. Cowpox inoculation had been tried before Jenner's time, from a country tradition of its preventive effect when casually acquired, but he it was who first thought of transmitting it from person to person by inoculation to build a population immune from endemic smallpox. He and his colleagues in the Gloucestershire Medical Society were the first medical men to prove the value of cowpox inoculation by subsequent variolation which took no effect; they tried swinepox and the similar 'grease' of horses also. Jenner's innovation was welcomed at first, but his excessive optimism with occasional mistakes and accidents soon attracted severe criticism which has continued into modern times. His confidence was vindicated at last when the World Health Organization announced in 1980 that smallpox had been eradicated from all countries by intensive vaccination campaigns, particularly in Africa, Asia and South America.

Jenner and his contemporaries knew nothing about the constitution of pox diseases except that their 'matter', the exudate from their lesions, was a pathogenic poison or virus in the Latin terminology of the time. The interrelation of the different poxes was observed and tested but not understood. Bacteria, seen in the 1680s, were rediscovered long after Jenner's death, and viruses in the modern sense were first differentiated as living organisms in 1892. Jenner's application of the general term virus to the pox exudates was a first step to this further specialization of the word. Medical scientists are attempting to produce synthetic vaccines effective against bacterial and virus infections which resist normal Jennerian vaccines, and report some success with experimental animals (*Nature*, 305 (1983), no. 5929).

As vaccination slowly spread through the world, research has been intensified at various times into the sources and relationship of the different strains of vaccine employed. Dr Derrick Baxby of Liverpool, a virologist particularly involved in this research, has given a very clear account of the history in the final chapter of his excellent book *Jenner's Smallpox Vaccine* (1981). The main part of his book is a detailed survey and critique of Jenner's work and controversies, so far as the written record of events from nearly two centuries past can be checked against knowledge acquired in the laboratory. While not uncritical of Jenner, he notes with mild amusement those critics who have supported their possibly justifiable dislike of vaccination by personal abuse of its originator, and endorses Jenner's good faith and 'his ideas far in advance of contemporary medical thought'.

Two years before he published his book Jenner inoculated a boy of eight, James Phipps, on 14 May 1796 with matter from the arm of Sarah Nelmes, a milkmaid who had contracted cowpox directly from an infected cow. Subsequently Jenner discussed his work with his friends, both medical and lay. On 19 July 1796 he wrote to Edward Gardner, a wine merchant and amateur poet, about this experiment: 'Now listen to the most delightful part of my story, the Boy has since been inoculated for

29

the small pox, which as I ventured to predict produc'd no effect'. Jenner recorded in his *Inquiry* (p. 54) that he sent an account of his investigations to Everard Home in London. Home, seven years younger than Jenner, was John Hunter's brother-in-law; he had been Hunter's assistant and was now a trustee of his Museum. He was making a great name as a surgeon and a comparative anatomist. Home sent Jenner's paper to Sir Joseph Banks on 21 April 1797 and was also given information about cowpox by the President of the Board of Agriculture. There is no formal record that the paper was offered to the Royal Society, but Jenner wrote to James Moore in 1809 'my paper was not with Sir Joseph, it was with Home . . . it was shewn to the Council and returned to me'.

Two preliminary drafts for the *Inquiry* have been preserved. One is a fair copy in Jenner's hand, inscribed by him 'On the Cow-pox, the original paper'. The other was written for him, probably by his nephew William Davies; it was signed and dated by Jenner 'March 29th, 1797' with a few notes and additions of his own; his autograph dedication to C. H. Parry dated 'July 10th, 1797' is inserted at the beginning, and there are a few pencilled suggestions in Parry's hand.

Both drafts were written in 1797, but Baron (1827) wrote that cowpox disappeared from Berkeley that year; Paul Saunders (1982) has suggested that Jenner made little advance in his research, preoccupied through the year in attending Lady Berkeley during a long illness. He was busy with vaccinations in the spring of 1798 and, according to Baron, then prepared his work for the press, again consulting a group of friends. The latest inoculations recorded in the printed book are of April 1798. On 24 April Jenner took this final draft to London, where it was published about midsummer, with the dedication to Parry now dated 21 June 1798. Jenner left London on 14 July, and reached Cheltenham in the evening of the same day.

*An Inquiry into Cow-Pox* is partly a discursive essay and partly a clinical treatise. After two paragraphs of philosophic generalization, Jenner described the pox disease of horses known as 'grease' and then gave his opinion that 'the disease makes its progress as I conceive to the nipple of the cow and from the cow to the human subject . . . What renders the cow-pox virus so extremely singular is that the person who has been thus affected is for ever after secure from the infection of the smallpox'. He next records the accurate observation that 'pustulous sores frequently appear on the nipples of the cow of a much milder nature than the true cowpox. This disease is incapable of producing any specific effects on the human constitution'. Here Jenner has expressed his three main conclusions:

(1) The cow must acquire the virus from the horse before passing it to the human.

(2) Cowpox virus gives the human patient permanent protection against smallpox.

(3) Only 'true' cowpox gives this protection.

All three conclusions he modified later in the light of further experience but, in doing so rather awkwardly, he brought severe criticism on his honesty as well as on his investigations; this criticism has been revived several times in the succeeding two centuries. Worst of all was his handling of the distinction between 'true and spurious cowpox', which his antagonists assumed to be a mere cover for mistakes. Baxby (1981, chapter 10) has discussed this in detail, commenting, in his vindication of Jenner's observation, that 'this subject shows us Jenner at his most brilliant and his most evasive'.

The evidence is set out in twenty-three case histories: Cases 1–12 are of casually acquired cowpox which afforded immunity from smallpox; several of these include more than one patient. Cases 13–15 are records of immunity after horsepox. Case 16, with plate 1, is that of Sarah Nelmes, from whom Jenner inoculated Case 17, 'a boy', with cowpox on 14 May 1796. Case 18 is an inoculation with horsepox from a man to a boy in March 1798, illustrated on plate 2. Case 19 records the inoculation of a boy with cowpox direct from the cow, and thence from his arm to another boy (Case 20 and plate 3), and from the latter to several children and adults (including Case 21 with plate 4) and then to several others (Cases 22 and 23) during March and April 1798.

In a footnote to Case 4 Jenner describes his accurate observation of the phenomenon afterwards called anaphylaxis. It is the first notice of the condition. Jenner observed that in this case of Mary Barge, who had had cowpox, an extensive inflammation was produced at variolation in 1791: 'It is remarkable that variolous matter when the system is disposed to reject it should excite inflammation . . . more speedily than when it produces the smallpox . . . It seems as if a change, which endures through life, had been produced in the action, or disposition to action, in the vessels of the skin . . . Whether this change has been effected by the Small Pox or the Cow Pox the disposition to sudden cuticular inflammation is the same on the application of variolous matter'.

This clear explanation of the appearances was not corroborated for nearly forty years, when François Magendie demonstrated it experimentally (1839); biochemical analysis came as late as 1902 from

P. Portier and C. Richet, who introduced the term 'anaphylaxie'. From consideration of this excessive antibody reaction to immunological intervention Clemens von Pirquet at Vienna formed his concept of natural hypersensitivity, which he named 'Allergie' in a paper in the *Münchener medizinische Wochenschrift* (1906) and treated more fully in his book *Klinische Studien über Vakzination und vakzinale Allergie* (1907) beginning with the words 'Vaccination, which we owe to that man of genius Jenner, is still our best method of immunizing'. Jenner's observation was thus an anticipation of the science of allergy.

*An Inquiry into Cow-Pox* is completed with 'General Observations'. Jenner admitted that the origin of cowpox from 'grease' in horses was not proved from actual experiments. He believed, however, that the virus from the horse's heels greatly increased in 'active quality' after it had acted upon the nipples of the cow. He suspected that the virus would possibly not affect the sound skin of the human body. He recorded a case showing that cowpox, while it gives immunity against smallpox, does not prevent repeated cowpox infection. He thought that the virus when taken from the horse is 'undetermined and uncertain in its effects', but that after passing through the cow it 'invariably and completely' possesses the specific properties which 'effect in the human constitution that peculiar change which forever renders it unsusceptible of the variolous contagion'. He speculated as to the compound origin of other infectious diseases; and discussed the varying severity of smallpox epidemics. Jenner then dealt with the technical aspect of inoculation: the need for attention to the state of the variolous matter, and the danger of inoculating too deep. He maintained that the method of inoculation is more important than .the general treatment.

After discussing the dangers of variolous inoculation, Jenner introduced his main proposal: 'As I have never known fatal effects from cowpox and as it clearly appears that the disease leaves the constitution in a state of perfect security from the infection of the smallpox, may we not infer that a mode of inoculation may be introduced preferable to that at present adopted'. He shows from three cases that cowpox cannot be propagated by effluvia. After three more case histories, one of which demonstrates the existence of 'true' and 'spurious' cowpox, he admits that conjecture has been occasionally admitted in an inquiry founded on experiment, in order to present his readers with objects for a more minute investigation. 'In the meantime I shall myself continue to prosecute this inquiry, encouraged by the pleasing hope of its becoming essentially beneficial to mankind'.

Jenner's achievement was well assessed by Dr Thomas Bradley, who discussed the *Inquiry* at length in the first issue of his *Medical and Physical Journal* (March 1799). His review concluded: 'Although Dr Jenner does not claim the discovery of the cowpox or the effects of it in preventing the smallpox when taken naturally, he is undoubtedly entitled to all the merit and honour of having brought the subject of inoculating it completely before the public, and directed the attention of the profession in general to an investigation of its truth and importance'.

In April 1799 Jenner issued from the same press his *Further Observations* (52); the two pamphlets were translated into Latin (38) and German (39) during this year. Early in 1800 he published *A Continuation* (58). This was also issued, combined with the two previous books, as the second edition of the *Inquiry* (24) with a new dedication to King George III dated 20 December 1799; a copy was presented to the King on 7 March 1800 and is now in the British Library.

Soon after the *Inquiry* was published, Benjamin Waterhouse at Boston received a copy from J. C. Lettsom and made the first vaccinations in North America early in 1799. Jenner sent a copy to his friend John Clinch in Newfoundland, where he had settled in 1786; Clinch became an active vaccinator from at least 1800. The copies sent to Waterhouse and to Clinch are now in the Countway Library of Medicine at Boston.

A French translation of the first two pamphlets, made by J. J. de Laroque in February 1800, was printed without his consent during the year; about 1805 he published his own revised and enlarged edition. Luigi Careno, who had already made a Latin translation, published an Italian version in 1800; a Dutch translation appeared in 1801, and a Portuguese in 1803.

Jenner's third edition, textually the same as the second but with minor corrections, was printed by Low's successor Shury in 1801. An American edition was published in 1802 at Springfield, Massachusetts. Though vaccination spread widely, smallpox epidemics continued to break out. In the campaign against them the *Inquiry* was reissued in Italy in 1853, and in Australia and the United States in 1884. Careno's Italian translation was reprinted in 1853 in a 'second edition corrected and enlarged by an appendix and a proposal of general maxims recommended to Governments to exstirpate the "arab contagion" radically' by Dr G. M. Goldoni, curator of vaccine lymph at Modena. The Australian reprint of Jenner's second edition (1884) was published by the Government of New South Wales at the instigation of George Bennett FRCS after a catastrophic smallpox epidemic in 1881–82, to instruct local authorities and medical men. It was printed from Bennett's copy (now in the Mitchell Library at

Sydney) and is a careful reproduction, not 'a perfect facsimile' as the preface claims; Sir Edward Ford has recounted its history in the *Medical Journal of Australia*, 2 (1951), 320–24.

The American reprint of the *Inquiry, Further Observations* and *Continuation* was published by Dr Joseph Jones, President of the Louisiana State Board of Health in his official book *Contagious and Infectious Diseases . . . for the guidance of the quarantine officers and sanitary inspectors* (1884). Joseph Jones served as an army surgeon through the Civil War and published *Spurious Vaccination in the Confederate Army* in 1867. During a tour of Europe he collected early vaccination books; his copies of Jenner's first, second and third editions, in the Library of the Medical Society of the County of King's, Brooklyn, New York, are inscribed by him 'London, September 6, 1870'. His son Dr Stanhope Bayne Jones told me in 1950 that his father's books and pioneer collection of Indian antiquities from the Southern States were sold soon after his death.

E. M. Crookshank published his *History and Pathology of Vaccination* in 1889 while Professor of Bacteriology at King's College, London. The book was intended to publicize the danger of vaccination, because he was justifiably sceptical of some vaccines in current use. Distrusting the veracity of Jenner's writings, he disparaged Jenner's character and, as evidence for these opinions, included in his book the text of the 1798 *Inquiry* with the variants from the autograph draft and the third edition, and the text of *Further Observations*. An unsigned article in the *British Medical Journal* (1896), written probably by J. B. Bailey, librarian of the Royal College of Surgeons, showed the inaccuracy of Crookshank's reading of the autograph draft which belongs to the College.

Since the centenary in 1896 of Jenner's first successful vaccination, the text of the *Inquiry* has been reprinted or reproduced in facsimile at least ten times. The case histories in the *Inquiry* are discussed in detail by Baxby (1981).

## MANUSCRIPTS

*Inquiry*    Manuscript 1: Royal College of Surgeons of England.

In Edward Jenner's hand. 4°:30 leaves in twos, the last 5 blank. Leaf 1a: 'On the Cowpox, the original paper'; 1b blank: 2a–25a Text, headed 'An Inquiry into the natural History of a Disease known in Glostershire by the name of the Cow-pox' ['by' *written above* 'under']; Leaves 11 (single) and

*An Inquiry into the natural History of a Disease known in Glostershire ~~under~~ by the name of the Cow-pox*

The deviations of Man from the state in which he was originally plac'd by Nature seem to have proved to him a prolific source of Diseases. From the love of Splendor, from the indulgences of Luxury, & from his fondness for amusement, he ~~has~~ familiariz'd himself with a great number of animals ~~that~~ which may not originally have been intended for his associates. The Wolf, disarm'd of ~~its~~ ferocity, is now pillow'd in the Lady's lap.* The Cat, the little Tygger of

_____

The late Mr. John Hunter proved by experiments that the Dog is the Wolf in a degenerated state

On the Cow-pox (Manuscript 1)

35

12–13 interpolated, 20 is also single; leaves 2b–13a paged as 2–23, leaf 13b blank, leaf 14a paged as 21; leaves 14a–25a, originally paged 22–43, corrected to 24–45; leaves 25b–30b blank. Eleven cases were recorded at first, no. 5 was altered to 6 and a new 5 and 7 inserted, with the remainder renumbered to 13.

Bought by Sir James Paget FRS from Jenner's descendants and presented to the Royal College of Surgeons, of which he was a past President, in 1879.

*Inquiry*   Manuscript 2: Wellcome Institute Library.

In the hand of Jenner's nephew William Davies the younger, with additions by Jenner and pencilled notes by C. H. Parry. 4°:1 leaf, 44 pages, 2 leaves. Leaf 1: Jenner's autograph dedication to C. H. Parry, July 10th 1797; pp. 1–44 Text, headed 'An Inquiry into the natural History of a Disease known in ["the western Counties of England particularly" *added by Jenner*] Glostershire under ["by" *superscribed*] the name of Cow-pox'; p. 44 at end of text 'Edwd Jenner. Berkeley, Glostershire. March 29th 1797'; 2 final leaves in Jenner's hand.

Bought by Sir Henry Wellcome from the Mockler collection of Jenner family papers at Sotheby's in 1918. For a full description see S. A. J. Moorat *Catalogue of Western Manuscripts on Medicine and Science in the Wellcome Historical Medical Library* II (1) (1973), no. 3019.

The manuscripts vary from each other and from the printed text. They cannot be dated precisely because leaves have been interpolated in each. The latest case history in MS 1 is of 28 March 1797, the day before completion of MS 2, while some interpolations in MS 2 seem to be copied from MS 1; possibly Jenner dictated MS 2 before writing MS 1. I collated them in 1948 before Moorat made his fuller collation of MS 2; Dr Baxby has collated them again very recently and I am indebted to him for the revision; he tells me that the name 'Variola vaccina' is not in either manuscript, nor is the differentiation of 'true' and 'spurious' cowpox, though 'different types' are mentioned in one place.

## Printed Editions

**23[20]** An Inquiry into the Causes and Effects of the Variolae Vaccinae, a disease discovered in some of the western counties of England, particularly Gloucestershire, and known by the name of the Cow Pox. [*double rule*] By Edward Jenner, M.D. F.R.S. &c. [*double rule*] — Quid nobis certius ipsis sensibus esse potest, quo vera ac falsa notemus. Lucretius. [*double rule*] London: Printed, for the Author, by Sampson Low, No. 7, Berwick Street, Soho; and sold by Law, Ave-Maria Lane; and Murray and Highley, Fleet Street. [*Ornament*] 1798.

COLLATION: 4°:A⁴(−A4), B–K⁴, L⁴(−L4):1 l, iv, 75 pp., 1 l; 4 coloured plates. 275 mm.

CONTENTS: A1ᵃ Half-title; [*double rule*] An Inquiry into the Causes and Effects of the Variolae Vaccinae. [*double rule*] Price 7s. 6d.; A2ᵃ Title; A3ᵃ⁻ᵇ, pp. [iii]–iv [Dedication] To C. H. Parry, M.D. at Bath, June 21st, 1798; B1ᵃ–B4ᵃ, pp. 1–7 Text, headed: An Inquiry &c. &c.; C1ᵃ–G2ᵇ, pp. 9–44: Case I–[XXIII]; G3ᵃ–L2ᵃ, pp. 45–75: I shall now conclude this Inquiry with some general observations . . .; L3ᵃ Errata.

PLATES: Nos. 1–4 facing pp. 32 (E4ᵇ), 36 (F2ᵇ), 38 (F3ᵇ), 40 (F4ᵇ); no. 1: *W. Skelton delt. et sculpt.*, nos. 2–4 *Edwd. Pearce delt. Willm. Skelton sculpt.*

NOTE: According to the 'Advertisement', inserted in the second edition of the Inquiry, the first edition was published in June 1798. The semi-colons following Soho and Lane in the imprint are anomalous types, (1) comma over x, (2) x over comma.

COPIES USED: BL, LSH, RCP, RCS, WHM.

INSCRIBED COPIES: RCP: "Dr. Simms from his obliged Friend the Author"; Crummer (Michigan University): "Thos. Westfaling Esq., from his obliged Friend the Author"; Countway Library, Boston: "For the Rev. John Clinch from his affectionate Friend the Author".

**24[21]** An Inquiry into the causes and effects of the Variolae Vaccinae, a disease discovered in some of the western counties of England, particularly Gloucestershire, and known by the name of the Cow Pox [*Double rule*] By Edward Jenner, M.D. F.R.S. &c. [*Double rule*] — Quid nobis certius ipsis sensibus esse potest, quo vera ac falsa notemus. Lucretius. [*Double rule*] Second Edition. [*Double rule*] London: Printed, for the

AN

# *INQUIRY*

INTO

## THE CAUSES AND EFFECTS

OF

## THE VARIOLÆ VACCINÆ,

### A DISEASE

DISCOVERED IN SOME OF THE WESTERN COUNTIES OF ENGLAND,

PARTICULARLY

## *GLOUCESTERSHIRE,*

AND KNOWN BY THE NAME OF

## THE COW POX.

---

BY EDWARD JENNER, M. D. F. R. S. &c.

---

——— QUID NOBIS CERTIUS IPSIS
SENSIBUS ESSE POTEST, QUO VERA AC FALSA NOTEMUS.

LUCRETIUS.

---

London:

PRINTED, FOR THE AUTHOR,

BY SAMPSON LOW, Nº. 7, BERWICK STREET, SOHO:

AND SOLD BY LAW, AVE-MARIA LANE; AND MURRAY AND HIGHLEY, FLEET STREET.

1798.

An Inquiry into Cowpox (First edition 1798)

38

Author, by Sampson Low, No. 7, Berwick Street, Soho: and sold by Law, Ave Maria Lane; and Murray and Highley, Fleet Street. [*Rule*] 1800.

COLLATION: 4°:(A)–R⁴, S², χ², χ–2A⁴, 2B²:vii, 182 pp. 1 l; 4 plates, 265 mm. K2 is a cancel, signed K2ˣ; K2ˣᵇ is paged:[2].

CONTENTS: A1ᵃ Half-title [*double rule*] An Inquiry &c. &c. [*double rule*]; A2ᵃ Title; A3ᵃ–A4ᵃ [Dedication]: To the King, dated Dec. 20th 1799; B1ᵃ–I4ᵇ, pp. 1–64. Text of An Inquiry; K1ᵃ Half-title of Further Observations on the Variolae Vaccinae; K2ˣ ᵃ⁻ᵇ Advertisement; K3ᵃ–T2ᵃ, pp. [69]–139 text of Further Observations; T3ᵃ Half-title of A continuation of Facts and Observations relative to the Variolae Vaccinae; T4ᵃ Title of A Continuation . . . 1800; T5ᵃ–2B1ᵇ, pp. [145]–182 text of A Continuation; 2B1ᵇ colophon: [*double rule*] Printed by Sampson Low, Berwick Street, Soho; 2B2ᵃ Errata.

PLATES: Nos. 1–4 facing pp. 30, 34, 36, 38; no. 1: *W. Skelton delt et scult. Cold. by W. Cuff*; nos. 2–4: *Edwd. Pearce delt. Cold. by W. Cuff. Wllm. Skelton sculpt*.

NOTE: Some copies are on blue paper watermarked 98: other copies on white paper watermarked 1798. The Advertisement to Further Observations states: The foregoing pages contain the whole of my first Treatise on the Variolae Vaccinae published in June 1798 . . . I was induced to offer to the world Further observations . . . published in the beginning of the year 1799. These treatises I have here combined, together with some additions.

COPIES USED: BL, RCP, RCS, WHM.

INSCRIBED COPIES: Crummer, Michigan University, on half-title: "Edw. Jenner, Bond Street"; OLM "Dr. Macintosh"; BmMI "For Henry Hicks Esq. from his obliged Friend the Author", subsequently in possession of Dr John Baron: CLM, a gift from Jenner to Dr John Jeffries, with corrections and notes in Jenner's hand, that on p. 125 signed "E.J."; BL copy from library of King George III to whom this edition is dedicated; Mitchell Library, Sydney: George Bennett's copy, see **27**.

**25[22]**   An Inquiry . . . [*waved rule*] The Third Edition [*waved rule*]. London: Printed for the Author, by D. N. Shury, No. 7, Berwick Street, Soho; and sold by Hurst, Paternoster Row; Murray and Highley, Fleet Street; Carpenter, Old Bond Street; and Callow, Crown Court. [*rule*] 1801.

COLLATION: 4°:A–T⁴, X–Z⁴, 2A⁴, 2B⁴(–2B4):vii, 182 pp.:4 plates, 283 mm. K2ᵇ paged[68].

CONTENTS: As in **24** except: K2 is a normal leaf: X1ᵃ–2B3ᵇ, pp. [145]–182 text of A Continuation . . .; 2B3ᵇ, p. 182 colophon: [*double rule*] Printed by D. N. Shury, Berwick Street, Soho.

PLATES: Nos. 1–4 face pp. 30, 34, 36, 38.

COPIES USED: BL, LSH, RCS, StBH, WHM.

## NOTE ON THE TEXT OF FIRST, SECOND, AND THIRD EDITIONS

Minor variations of type or spelling (e.g. Cow Pox or Cow-Pox) are not noticed.

Text occupies: (1) 163 × 126 mm, (2) 171 × 119 mm, (3) 169 × 121 mm.

P. 5 (1) shiverings with general lassitude, (2) and (3) shiverings, succeeded by heat, general lassitude . . .

(1) needlessly, (2) and (3) heedlessly.

P. 6 (1) from the Horse to the nipple, (2) and (3) Horse (as I conceive) . . .

P. 7 (1) disease is not be considered, (2) is not considered, (3) is not to be considered.

P. 7 footnote of (1) incorporated into text of (2) and (3).

P. 17 of (3), misprinted 'preceeing'.

P. 22 footnote lengthened in (2) p. 21, and further lengthened in (3) p. 21.

P. 23 of (2), line 4 misprinted 'produced the the least'.

P. 24 (1) sore, (2) and (3) p. 23 tumour.

P. 29 of (3) footnote added.

P. 31 of (2) and (3) footnote added.

P. 35 (1) blueish, (2) and (3) bluish.

P. 38 of (3) footnote added.

P. 40 (1) Macklove, (2) and (3) Marklove.

P. 40 of (2) a third footnote added.

P. 41 (1) scepticus, (2) and (3) septicus.

P. 43 (1) this boy and William, (2) and (3) this boy (Barge) . . .

P. 42 (1) pustule, an appearance, (2) and (3) pustule, and appearance.

P. 45 (1) Dolland, (2) and (3) Dollan.

P. 47 of (2) additional footnote.

P. 60 (1) moderate, (2) and (3) p. 54 modern.

P. 57 of (3) footnote omitted.

P. 60 of (3) footnote added.

P. 61 of (3) footnote added.

P. 64 of (2) and (3) catchword FURTHER.

P. 116 of (2) and (3) conversation, wrongly for 'observation' in Further Observations (1799) p. 48.

**26[23]**     An Inquiry into the Causes and Effects of the Variolae Vaccinae, a disease discovered in some of the western counties of England, particularly Gloucestershire, and known by the name of the Cow Pox [*double rule*] By Edward Jenner, M.D. F.R.S. &c. [*double rule*] — Quid nobis certius ipsis sensibus esse potest, quo vera ac falsa notemus. Lucretius. [*double rule*] From the Second London Edition. [*double rule*] Springfield: Re-printed for Dr. Samuel Cooley, by Ashley & Brewer. [*ornament*] 1802.

COLLATION: 8°:(A⁴)–P⁴:iv, 116 pp.:4 plates. 150 mm.

CONTENTS: p. [i] Title; pp. [iii]–iv, To the King; pp. [1]–42, An Inquiry, &c. [*between rules*]; pp. 43–91, Further Observations; pp. 92–116 A Continuation.

PLATES: between pp. 18–19, 22–23, 24–25, 26–27.

COPIES: CLM, LC, LML, MSK, NLM, NWU, NYAM (2), YMH.

# INQUIRY

INTO

*THE CAUSES AND EFFECTS*

OF THE

*VARIOLÆ VACCINÆ,*

A DISEASE

Difcovered in fome of the weftern counties
of England,

PARTICULARLY GLOUCESTERSHIRE,

And known by the name of

# THE COW POX.

BY *EDWARD JENNER,* M. D. F. R. S. &c.

———— *Quid nobis certius ipfis
Senfibus effe poteft, quo vera ac falfa notemus.*
LUCRETIUS.

FROM THE SECOND LONDON EDITION.

SPRINGFIELD :

RE-PRINTED FOR DR. *SAMUEL COOLEY,*

BY ASHLEY & BREWER.

1802.

An Inquiry into Cowpox (Springfield, Massachusetts 1802)

42

**27[24]**     An Inquiry [as second edition, to] 1800, 3a 134–84.

COLLATION: 4°:[A]1–5, B–Z⁴, 2A², 2B1:v, 184 pp.:4 plates, 264 mm. A1, A2 and A5 single leaves; A3–A4 conjugate.

CONTENTS: A1ᵃ Title; A1ᵇ [*rule*] Reprinted by Authority: Thomas Richards, Government Printer, Sydney, 1884; A2ᵃ Preface; A3ᵃ–A4ᵃ [Dedication] To the King; A5ᵃ–I4ᵃ, pp. 1–65 Text; K1ᵃ Half-title of Further Observations; K2ᵃ⁻ᵇ Advertisement; K3ᵃ–T2ᵃ, pp. 71–141 text of Further Observations; T2ᵃ Half-title of A Continuation; T4ᵃ Title of A Continuation; U1ᵃ–2B1ᵇ, pp. 147–184 text of A Continuation; 2B1ᵇ, p. 184 [five lines of text] . . . Finis [*double rule*] Printed by Sampson Low, Berwick Street, Soho.

PLATES: Lithographed, without lettering, face p. 30, 34, 36, 38.

NOTE: Described in the preface as 'a perfect facsimile' of the second edition: but while the title-page follows the layout of the 1800 edition, and the book is approximately the same size, the arrangement of the text is new, and the plates have been re-drawn. Errors in the text have been tacitly corrected at pp. 7, 9, 24, 41 and 118, and there are variations of spelling or punctuation at pp. 15, 33, 34, 47 and 48. There is no catchword on p. 65, no half-title, no errata leaf, and the long s is not used.

COPIES: Canberra: National Library; Melbourne: PL, UL, Australian Medical Association, RACS, K. F. Russell; Sydney: PL (2), Mitchell Library, RACP; London: RCS; Montreal: OLM (*Bibliotheca Osleriana* 1253); Uppsala: UL (Erik Waller collection).

COPIES USED: RCS and one lent by F. Wood Jones FRS in 1948.

**28[25]**     Contagious and infectious diseases, measures for their prevention and arrest. Smallpox (variola); modified smallpox (varioloid); chickenpox (varicella); cow-pox (variolae vaccinae); vaccination, spurious vaccination. Illustrated by eight coloured plates. [*rule*] Circular no. 2, prepared for the guidance of the quarantine officers and sanitary inspectors of the Board of Health of the State of Louisiana. By Joseph Jones M.D., President of the Board of Health of the State of Louisiana. [*rule*] (Extract from the Report of the Board of Health to the General Assembly of Louisiana, 1883, 1884. [*rule*] Baton Rouge. Printed by Leon Jastremski, State printer. 1884.

COLLATION: 8°: no signatures: viii, 410 pp.: plates 17–24. 226 mm.

NOTE: Title, p. i, dated 1884; half-title, p. 1, 1883. The plates are by The New Orleans Lith. Co. 10 Union Street. The bracket before 'Extract' on title page has no complementary bracket.

JENNER CONTENTS: P. 10: Title and preface of 1800; pp. 11–56 text of 1801 (Inquiry, Further observations, and A Continuation) with pseudo-facsimiles of the title page of Inquiry 3rd ed. (p. 11), the half-title of Further observations (p. 29) and the title page of A Continuation (p. 47). Pp. 12, 28, 30, 46 and 48 blank. Jenner's plate 1 is reproduced as plate 17, fig. 76, facing p. 20, and his plates 2, 3 and 4 as plate 18, figs. 77, 78 and 79 facing p. 22. Pp. 57–59: Dr. Jenner's Account of the Origin of the vaccine inoculation (The Medical Repository, vol. v, p. 239, New York, 1802). Pp. 59–61: Dr. Jenner's instructions for vaccine inoculation – The Medical Repository, vol. v, New York, 1802;p. 483.

COPY USED: RCS presented by the Author.

**29[26]** History and Pathology of Vaccination. Vol. II. Selected Essays edited by Edgar M. Crookshank, M.B., Professor of Comparative Pathology and Bacteriology, and Fellow of King's College, London. Author of papers on the etiology of scarlet fever; anthrax in swine; tuberculosis and the public milk supply; and the history and pathology of actinomycosis; in reports of the Agricultural department of the Privy Council. Author of 'A Manual of Bacteriology', etc. London, H. K. Lewis, 136 Gower Street, W.C. 1889. (All rights reserved).

COLLATION: 8°:vi, 610 pp., 251 mm. The Jenner texts occur as follows: p. 1 An Inquiry . . . [facsimile of 1798 half-title] Reprinted from the First Edition (1798). The readings in the MS of the Original Paper, and the corrections in the Third Edition (1801) will be found in footnotes – E.M.C.; p. 2 Title of the manuscript (From the Manuscript of the Original Paper in the Library of the Royal College of Surgeons, London – E.M.C.); p. 3 reduced facsimile of the 1798 title page; p. 5 dedication To Parry; p. 6 dedication To the King; pp. 7–33 text of Inquiry; [Jenner's four plates are reproduced (lithographs by Vincent Brooks, Day and Son) in Crookshank's vol. I as plates 2, 4, 5 and 6 facing respectively pp. 136, 272, 274 (both 5 and 6), plate 4 facing p. 272 is entered in the list of contents as plate 3 facing p. 248 which is not one of Jenner's plates]; pp. 155–89 text of Further Observations with reproduction of 1799 title; no half-title; pp. 247–66 text of A Continuation, with reproduction of title and half-title of 1801; pp. 267–274 text of The Origin . . . 1801.
Also issued in America with Philadelphia imprint.

COPY USED: RCS.

**30[27]** Medical and Surgical Memoirs . . . By Joseph Jones . . . New Orleans, L. Graham for the author, 1890. 3 volumes.

CONTENTS: Vol. 3, part I, pp. 135–542 contain the text of his Contagious Diseases 1883–84 (**28**) with new pagination; Jenner's texts occur as follows: pp. 143–59 with plates 17–18 Inquiry; pp. 161–77 Further Observations; pp. 179–88 A Continuation; pp. 189–91 The Origin; pp. 191–3 Instructions.

COPY USED: RCS.

**31[28]**    An Inquiry into the causes and effects of the Variolae Vaccinae, a disease discovered in some of the western counties of England, particularly Gloucestershire, and known by the name of the Cow Pox [*rule*] By Edward Jenner, M.D. F.R.S. &c. [*rule*] — Quid nobis certius ipsis sensibus esse potest, quo vera ac falsa notemus. Lucretius. [*rule*] London: Printed for the Author, by Sampson Low, No. 7 Berwick Street, Soho: and sold by Law, Ave-Maria Lane; and Murray and Highley, Fleet Street. 1798. Republished by Cassell and Company, Limited, 1896.

COLLATION: 8°:p. 9 signed ★, p. 17 signed ★★; 36 pp., 188 mm.

CONTENTS: P. (1) Title; (2) blank; (3) Preface to Reprint; (4) blank; (5) Dedication to C. H. Parry; (6) blank; 7–36 text. Grey paper wrappers: (1) As title page, headed: The Practitioner's Library of Medical Classics. [*rule*] No. 1. Price 1s. 6d. [*rule*] An Inquiry . . . republished by Cassell and Company, Limited, 1896; (2) blank; (3) Cassell's advertisements; (4) advertisement of The Jenner Centenary Number of The Practitioner . . . the May number . . . a handsome portrait of Dr. Jenner and Dr. Jenner's original paper.

COPY USED: BL.

NOTE: The preface states: 'The plates have not been reproduced . . . In hardly any two copies of the original edition is the colouring of the plates exactly alike . . . they were coloured by hand and . . . (owing apparently to the presence of lead in the pigment) the colour in some of them has become much darker than it was originally'. The editor of *The Practitioner* in 1896 was Sir Malcolm Morris (1849–1924).

**32[29]**    Epoch-making Contributions to Medicine, Surgery and the allied Sciences being reprints of those communications which first conveyed epoch-making observations to the scientific world together with biographical sketches of the observers collected by C. N. B. Camac, A.B., M.D. with portraits. Philadelphia and London, W. B. Saunders Company 1909.

COLLATION: 8°:x, 435 pp., 7 portraits.

JENNER CONTENTS: P. 205 half-title: Vaccination against Smallpox; facing p. 206 photographic reproduction of W. Ridley's engraving, October 1804, of North-cote's second portrait of Jenner [Chapter 8, III 6(i)]; pp. 207–11 Edward Jenner 1749–1803 [biographical sketch]; facing p. 212 photographic reproduction of title of Inquiry 1798; p. 213 half-title; p. 214 dedication To Parry: pp. 215–40 text of Inquiry; p. 241 half-title; p. 242 dedication; pp. 243–76 text of Further Obser-vations; p. 277 half-title; pp. 279–96 text of A Continuation; pp. 296–98 List of writings and editions.

COPY USED: RCS.

**33[30]**    The Three Original Publications on Vaccination against Small-pox by Edward Jenner, in The Harvard Classics edited by Charles W. Eliot LL.D. Scientific papers: Physiology, Medicine, Surgery, Geology with introduction, notes and illustrations. P. F. Collier & Son, New York (H C xxxviii, 1910), pp. 149–231.

CONTENTS: P. 149 half-title; p. 150 introductory note; p. 151 dedication To C. H. Parry; p. 153 Vaccination against Smallpox, I An Inquiry . . . 1798; p. 180 II Further Observations . . . 1799; p. 214 III A Continuation . . . 1800; p. 231 end of text.

NOTE: At p. 155 editor's note on erroneous identification of 'grease' and cowpox: facing p. 160 reproduction of Lawrence's portrait of Jenner.

COPY USED: BL.

**33A**    The same, reissued: New York 1938.

**33B**    The same, reissued: New York 1961.

**34[31]**    An Inquiry . . . [Facsimile of the first edition.] Milan 1923.

COLLATION: 4°: as first edition with additional leaves, blank at beginning and L4 at end. Plates face pp. 32, 36, 38 and 40.

CONTENTS: A1–L3 as first edition; L4ª 'This facsimile edition of An Inquiry into the Causes and Effects of the Variolae Vaccinae, 1798, by Edward Jenner was published in 1923 the centenary of Jenner's death in an edition limited to 500 copies by R. Lier & C. – Milan 7 Via Brera.' Green board covers, paper label on front: [in a double rule border] Edward Jenner An Inquiry into the Causes and Effects of the

Variolae Vaccinae London 1798; paper label on spine: Jenner [*double rule*] Inquiry 1798; grey board slip-case with label as on front cover with additional lettering: [*rule*] R. Lier & Co., Milan, Via Brera 7.

COPY USED: WHM.

NOTE: Facsimile of MS corrections at pp. 5, 24, 40, 41 and 60 in accordance with list of errata.

**34A**    The same, reissued without the slip-case and leaf L4, both of which carried Lier's imprint, but with a separate brief life of Jenner by Nolie Mumey, in the same format. Denver, Colorado: Range Press [1949].

COPY USED: RCS, the gift of Dr Nolie Mumey.

**35[32]**    An Inquiry . . . [The text of Jenner's autograph draft, Manuscript 1] *The Lancet*, London 1 (1923), 137–41. [Contributed by V. G. Plarr, Librarian of the Royal College of Surgeons of England].

**36**    An Inquiry . . . Abridged from a facsimile edition . . . 1923 . . . Milan. In Thomas Dale Brock, translator and editor, *Milestones in Microbiology* [Papers by various authors], pp. 121–25. Englewood Cliffs, N.J., Prentice-Hall, 1961. 8°.

**37**    An Inquiry . . . Facsimile reprint [of the first edition]. Pall Mall Classics, London. Dawsons of Pall Mall (1966). 4°.

**37A**    An Inquiry . . . Facsimile reprint (limited edition). Nottingham Court Press, London, 1984. 4°.

TRANSLATIONS

**38[33]**    Eduardi Jenneri, Med. D. et Reg. Scient. Acad. Soc. Disquisitio de caussis et effectibus variolarum vaccinarum. [*ornament*] Ex Anglico in Latinum conversa ab Aloysio Careno, M. et Ph.D. et Reg. Imp. Acad. Mantuanae, Societ. Patriot. Mediolanens. Reg. Taurin. Medicochirurg. in Helvetia, Senens. Venet. Socio. [*double rule*] Cum Fig. colorat. [*double rule*] Vindobonae, Apud Camesina 1799.

COLLATION: 4°:χ⁴, A–I⁴(–I4):viii, 70 pp.:4 plates. 255 mm.

CONTENTS: χ1ᵃ Title; χ1ᵇ Motto from Lucretius; χ2ᵃ–3ᵇ [*double rule*] Praefatio . . . Vindobonae die prima Septembris 1799; χ4ᵃ⁻ᵇ [*double rule*] Amico Optimo C. H. Parry . . . ; A1ᵃ–C3ᵃ, pp. [1]–23 [*double rule*] Disquisitio de Caussis et Effectu Variolarum Vaccinarum; C3ᵇ–E1ᵇ, pp. 24–34 [*double rule*] Bibliothèque Britannique. Non dubito . . . Odier annotationes . . . ; E2ᵃ, p. 35 [*double rule*] Ephemerides Medico-Chirurgicae Salisburgenses; E2ᵇ–3ᵇ, pp. 36–38 Huc usque clarissimi Odier et Diarii Salisburgensis annotationes . . . Nunc quae Vindobonae . . . observata fuere, exponenda supersunt; E4ᵃ, p. [39] half-title Pars Altera; E4ᵇ blank; F1ᵃ⁻ᵇ, pp. [41–42] [*double rule*] dedication to Parry . . . 5ta Aprilis, 1799; F2ᵃ–I3ᵇ, pp. [43]–70 Disquisitio de Natura et Effectu Variolarum Vaccinarum; plates no. 1–4, Edwd. Pearce delt. Joh. Neidl. sculpt.

COPY USED: BLO.

PLATES: Lithographed in red and brown by Joh. Neidl.

NOTE: Careno in his preface gives the references for his additional matter and says that he includes Further Observations and the plates by the advice of Ballhorn, whose German version (**39**) was about to come from the press.

**39[34]**    Eduard Jenners der Arzneywissenschaft Doktors und Mitglieds der Königl. Societät der Wissenschaften Untersuchungen über die Ursachen und Wirkungen der Kuhpocken einer Krankheit die man in einigen westlichen Provinzen Englands vorzüglich in Gloucestershire bemerkt hat [*rule*] — Quid nobis certius ipsis sensibus esse potest, quo vera ac falsa notemus. Lucretius. [*rule*] Aus dem Englischen übersezt von G. Fr. Ballhorn d.A.W.D. [*double rule*] Hannover bei den Gebrüdern Hahn. 1799.

COLLATION: 8°:[χ]¹⁰, A–C⁸, D²: 6 l. unnumbered, pp. [iii]–x, 4 l, pp. [1]–52; folding plate.

CONTENTS: [χ]1ª half-title; [χ]2ª Title; [χ]3ª⁻ᵇ, pp. iii–iv dedication to Parry; [χ]4ª
–6ᵇ, pp. v–x Vorbericht des Uebersetzers . . . 9 May 1799: [χ]7ª–10ᵇ Vorbericht
zur zweiten Ausgabe . . . 19 August 1799: A1ª–D2ᵇ text. One coloured plate
showing four stages of pustule.

COPIES USED: NLM, YMH.


**40**    Auszug aus Hr. Jenner's Abhandlung über die Natur und Wirkungen der Kuhpocken [translation of Jenner's case histories] in J. Eyerel
*Praktische Beyträge zur Geschichte der Kinderpocken und Kuhpocken*, Vienna
1800, pp. 9–60.


**41[36]**    Recherches sur les Causes et les Effets de la Variolae vaccinae,
Maladie découverte dans plusieurs comtés de l'Ouest de l'Angleterre,
notamment dans le comté de Gloucester, et connue aujourd'hui sous le
nom de Vérole de Vache. Par Edward Jenner, Doct. en Méd. Membre de
la Société Royale, etc., et traduit de l'anglais par M.L.C. de Lxxxxxx [*rule*]
Quid nobis certius ipsis Sensibus esse potest, quo vera ac falsa notemus.
Lucretius. [*rule*] A Lyon, Chez Reymann et Ce, Libraires, rue St Domi-
nique, No 73. [*rule*] 1800.

COLLATION: 8°:[χ]², A–C⁸, D⁶:2 leaves, 60 pp. 208 mm.

CONTENTS: [χ] 1ª Title; [χ]2ª A M. Duret D.M., A Annonay, Comme un Témoin-
age d'Estime et d'Amitié, le Traducteur 3 Mars 1800; [χ]2ᵇ, A C. Parry . . .;
A1ª–D6ᵇ, pp. 1–60 [*ornament*] Recherches . . .

COPIES USED: BL in a volume of French vaccination tracts of 1800–02; WHM.

NOTE: The translator's initials represent Monsieur le Comte de Laroque; notes by
the translator are added at p. 2 [ignorance of French equivalent for 'the grease'];
p. 25 [plates omitted because of cost and sufficience of text]; pp. 48–9 [case of
variolous virus losing its specific properties in practice of Dr C . . . , and his
inoculation of sheep in Languedoc]. Baron wrote that three editions of this
translation were issued in seven months. Laroque disowned this edition; see note
to **46**.


**42[38]**    Ricerche sulle Cause e sugli Effetti del Vajuolo delle Vacche
Malattia scoperta in alcune provincie occidentali dell' Inghilterra, e special-
mente nel Contado di Glowcester, e conosciuta sotto il nome di Cow-pox
del dott. Odoardo Jenner membro della Società Reale di Londra ec.

Traduzione dall' Inglese nell' Italiano corredata d'aggiunte, e d'una Relazione del vajuolo, che affetta le vacche in Lombardia. Del dott. Luigi Careno medico pratico in Vienna, corrispondente della R. J. Accademia Medico-Chirurgica Gioseffina di Vienna e della Bavaro-Palatina di Monaco, Socio delle Accademie di Mantova, di Torino, di Zurigo, di Siena, e di Venezia . . . quid nobis certius ipsis sensibus esse potest, quo vera ac falsa notemus. Lucretius. [ornament] Pavia 1800. [rule] Nella Stamperia Bolzani. Con permissione.

COLLATION: 12°:$\chi^6$, A–F$^{12}$, G$^{14}$; xii, 172 pp.; folding plate. 168 mm: [$\chi$1–2] unsigned, [$\chi$3–4] signed $\chi$2–3, C5 unsigned, C6 signed 5. Plate in red and brown, J. F. Saltzenberg, sc. in Hannover.

CONTENTS: $\chi$1$^a$ Title; $\chi$2$^a$ dedication to Val. Luigi Brera; $\chi$[3]$^{a-b}$, pp. v–vi dedication to Parry: $\chi$[4]$^a$–6$^b$, pp. vii–xii Prefazione del Traduttore . . . Vienna 2 Settembre 1799; A1$^a$–C7$^b$, pp. 1–62 text of Inquiry, no heading, begins: Infiniti sono i mali; C8$^a$–D10$^b$, pp. 63–92: Estratto [summaries of reviews and reports by Odier pp. 63–83, Salzburg Ephemerides pp. 83–86, Hufeland p. 86, Vienna professors pp. 86–92); D11$^a$, p. 93 dedication of Further Observations; D11$^b$–G11$^b$, pp. 94–166 Osservazioni ulteriori; G12$^a$–14$^a$, pp. 167–71 Del vajuolo, che infetta le vacche nella Lombardia. Relazione Del Dott. Luigi Careno; G14$^a$, p. 171 at foot: Fine; G14$^b$ p. 172 Errori Correzioni.

COPIES USED: BL, WHM.

NOTE: The additional matter is the same as in Careno's Latin translation of 1799.


**43[40]**    Onderzoek naar de Oorzaaken en Uitwerkselen der Variolae Vaccinae, eene Ziekte, in de Westelijke Gedeelten van Engeland ontdekt, Voornaamlijk in het Graafschap Gloucester, en aldaar bekend onder den naam van Koepokken; Door Edw. Jenner, Med. Doct. &c. in het Nederduitsch vertaald en met een Bijvoegsel vermeerderd, Door L. Davids, Med. Doct. te Rotterdam [rule] — Quid nobis certius ipsis Sensibus esse potest, quo vera ac falsa notemus. Lucretius. [rule/short rule] Met Plaaten. [short rule/ornament] Te Haarlem, Bij A. Loosjes, P. Z. MDCCCI.

COLLATION: 8°:[$\chi$]$^2$, [$\chi$–3$\chi$]$^8$, [4$\chi$]$^2$, A–C$^8$:2 l, 52 pp., 48 pp.; 4 coloured plates. 225 mm.

CONTENTS: [$\chi$]1$^a$ half-title: Onderzoek naar de Oorzaaken en Uitwerkselen der Variolae Vaccinae; [$\chi$]2$^a$ Title; $\chi$1$^{a-b}$, pp. 1–2 Bericht van der Vertaaler; [$\chi$]2$^a$– [4$\chi$]2$^b$, pp. 3–52 Staat der Vaccine, in ons Land; A1$^a$–C8$^b$, pp. 1–48 Onderzoek omtrent de Oorzaken en intwerking der Koepokken.

PLATES: Unnumbered, facing pp. 20, 24, 26 and 27: G. Kitsen sculpt, printed in black, brown-red, blue and yellow, each on a separate leaf, watermark Pieter with crown device.

COVERS: Blue-grey paper on thin board: front cover lettered in a floriated border: E. Jenners Onderzoek, naar de Oorzaaken en Uitwerkselen der Variolae Vaccinae [rule] met Gekleurde Plaaten [rule], back cover in floriated border: de Plaaten te Plaatzen . . . ; lettered down spine: E. Jenner, Variolae Vaccinae.

COPY USED: MML.

NOTE: The translation includes Jenner's footnotes, and notes by 'Lat. Vertaaler' [Careno] and 'Vertaaler' [Davids].

**44[41]**    Baron 1 (1827), 393, stated that a Spanish translation was announced in 1801. No copy has been traced at Madrid or elsewhere, and it appears to be unknown to Spanish bibliographers.

**45[42]**    Indagaçao sobre as Causas, e Effeitos das Bexigas de Vacca, Molestia descoberta em alguns dos condados occidentaes da Inglaterra, particularmente na comarca de Gloucester, e conhecida pelo nome de Vaccina, por Eduardo Jenner, M.D. F.R.S. etc. — Quid nobis certius ipsis sensibus esse potest, quo vera ac falsa notemus. Lucretius. Segunda edição. Pubblicada em Londres em 1800. Traduzida do original Inglez por ordem de sua Alteza real o Principe Regente N.S. por J.A.M. [Royal arms] Lisboa, na Regia Officina Typographica. [rule] 1803.

COLLATION: 4°: [A]–R⁴, S1:137 pp.; 4 plates: folding plate. 235 mm.

CONTENTS: [A]1ᵃ Half-title: Indagaçao sobre as causas, e effeitos das bexigas de vacca; [A]2ᵃ Title; [A]3ᵃ⁻ᵇ dedication: Ao Rei; A4ᵃ–G1ᵇ, pp. [7]–50 Text of Inquiry; G2ᵃ half-title of Further Observations; G3ᵃ Advertencia; G4ᵃ–O1ᵇ, pp. 55–106, Ulteriores observações; O2ᵃ half-title of A Continuation; O3ᵃ Title of A Continuation; O4ᵃ–S1ᵃ, pp. 111–37, Continuaçao de factos, e observaçoes etc. etc.; S1ᵃ, p. 137 . . . Fim.

PLATES: 1–4 face pp. 26, 29, 31 and 32; nos. 1 and 3 signed DJS: Wa f; nos. 2 and 4: R J da Costa f; folding plate at end, recto: Quadro comparativo, verso: [list of Royal Jennerian Society] Traduzido pelo Dr. T. F. de Aguiar.

COPY USED: WHM.

**46[37]**     Oeuvres complètes du Docteur Jenner, membre de la Société Royale de Londres, etc. Sur la découverte de la vaccine, et tout ce qui concerne la pratique de ce nouveau mode d'inoculation [*rule*] Traduites de l'Anglais par Jacques-Joseph de Laroque au mois de février 1800. Nouvelle Edition revue, corrigée et considérablement augmentée. [*rule*] A Privas, de l'Imprimerie de F. Agard, Imprimeur de la Préfecture du département de l'Ardêche.

COLLATION: 8°:b$^8$, 1$^8$, 2$^4$, [$\star$]$^8$, B–P$^8$, Q1–5:lvi, 233 pp. 188 mm. B1–3 are signed as b1–3.

CONTENTS: b1$^a$ half-title: Oeuvres Complètes du Docteur Jenner; b2$^a$ title; b3$^a$–8$^a$, pp. v–xv Préface du Traducteur; I1$^a$–24a, pp. xvii–xxxix Mémoire sur la vaccine 20 Mai, 1804. Par M. Joseph de Laroque; [$\star$]1–8, pp. xli–lvi Supplément au Mémoire; B1$^a$–2$^b$ A M. Duret, D. M. à Annonay . . . [signed and dated] J. J. de Laroque, Londres, 3 Mars, 1800; B3$^{a-b}$ A C. Parry, D.M. à Bath; B4$^a$–F4$^a$, pp. 7–71 Recherches sur les causes et les effets de la petite vérole des vaches; F4$^b$–8$^b$, pp. 72–80 Seconde Lettre au Docteur Duret à Annonay; F8$^b$–G2$^b$, pp. 80–4 Lettre au Docteur Jenner, Londres, 5 Août, 1800 . . . [signed] J. J. de Laroque; G2$^b$–3$^a$, pp. 84–85 Reponse du Docteur Jenner, Cheltenham, comté de Glocester, 8 Août, 1800 [with note by Laroque to Duret, unsigned]; G3$^b$–5$^b$, pp. 86–90 Seconde Lettre du Docteur Jenner; G6$^a$–7$^a$, pp. 91–3 Seconde Lettre au Docteur Jenner, Londres, 21 Août, 1800; G7$^b$, p. 94 half-title and dedication of Further Observations: Observations Ultérieures sur la Vaccine, par Edward Jenner etc. 1799. Traduit de l'Anglais au mois de Mars 1800 [*rule*] [dedication to Parry]; G8$^a$–M5$^b$, pp. 95–170 Observations Ultérieures etc. etc. . . . ; M6$^a$–P6$^a$, pp. 171–221 Continuation De Faits et d'Observations sur la Vaccine, Août, 1800; P6$^b$ p. 222 Origine De l'Inoculation de la Vaccine, 6 Mai, 1801 [Jenner's preface]; P7$^a$–Q4$^b$, pp. 223–32 Origine De l'Inoculation de la Vaccine . . . ; Q4$^b$, p. 232 text ends . . . Fin; Q5$^a$, p. 233 Table des Matières Contenues dans ce Volume.

COPIES USED: WHM, WML(J).

NOTE: At p. xvii Laroque refers to his meeting with Jenner when leaving London in September 1803. At p. ix he speaks of the unauthorized version of his translation 'plein de fautes' printed for Dr Petit of Lyon and adds that Jenner gave him the privilege of translating *Further Observations, A Continuation*, and *The Origin*. The 'Supplément au Mémoire', pp. xli–lvi, not present in WHM copy, contains letters from M. Salet, Tournon, the second of which is dated 16 Janvier, 1805. (The late Dr Sanford V. Larkey, Director and Librarian of the Welch Medical Library, Baltimore, gave me these details of the Supplement). Privas lies more than 100 kilometres south of Lyon.

**47[39]** Ricerche sulle Cause e sugli Effetti del Vajuolo delle Vacche del Dottor Odoardo Jenner  Traduzione dall'Inglese corredata d'aggiunte e d'una relazione del vajuolo che affetta le vacche in Lombardia del Dottor Luigi Careno  Seconda Edizione corretta ed accresciuta di un' Appendice e d'una Proposta di massime generali raccomandate ai Governi onde radicalmente estirpare il contagio arabo del Dottor Gio. Michele Goldoni Conservatore della Linfa Vaccina in Modena [*ornament*] Modena Tip. di Antonio ed Angelo Cappelli 1853.

COLLATION: 12°:xviii, 144 pp.

COPY USED: NLM.

**48[43]** Izsledovanie prichin i posledovatelnago diystviya variolae vaccinae, bolezni, otkritoy v nikotovikh zapadnikh grafstvach Anglii, preimyshchestvenno v Gloucestershire i izvestnoy pod imenem korovei ospe, at pp. 372–97 of *Ospa i Ospoprivivanie* V. O. Guberta [Smallpox and vaccination by Vladislav Osipovich Hubert] vol. 1, St. Petersburg 1896, 533 pp.

CONTENTS: Russian translations of Jenner's texts: pp. 372–97 Inquiry; pp. 398–425 Further Observations; pp. 426–40 A Continuation; pp. 441–44 The Origin; pp. 445–50 Varieties and Modifications; pp. 450–52 Instructions; p. 493 Letter to Jenner from the Empress Marie Feodorovna 10 August 1802: pp. 494–95 Jenner's answer to the Empress 10 October 1802.

ILLUSTRATIONS: P. 371 title page of Inquiry 1798; plates 1–4 face pp. 384, 386, 388 and 390.

NOTE: Hubert's contributions include a history of smallpox, a translation of Rhazes and a life of Jenner with reproductions of 36 portraits. No further volume seems to have been published.

COPY USED: RSM.

**48A** Pocken und Pockenimpfung bei verschiedenen Volkern (Erlaüternden Text zur russischen Auflage) von Dr. Med. Wladislaw Hubert. St. Petersburg 1896. [German resumé of Hubert's text, omitting the translations from Jenner.]

COPY USED: YMH (A. C. Klebs collection).

**49[35]**     Klassiker der Medizin herausgegeben von Karl Sudhoff [*waved rule*] Edward Jenners Doktors der Medizin, Mitgliedes der Königl. Gesellschaft der Wissenchaften usw. Untersuchungen über die Ursachen und Wirkungen der Kuhpocken (1798) Übersetzt und eingeleitet von Prof. Dr. Viktor Fossel [*device*] Leipzig Verlag von Johann Ambrosius Barth 1911.

COLLATION: $8°$:$1-2^8$, $3^4$:38 pp., 1 blank leaf. 192 mm.

CONTENTS: $1_1{}^a$ title: $1_1{}^b$ motto from Lucretius, at foot Druck von Metzger und Wittig in Leipzig: $1_2{}^a-4^b$, pp. 3–8 Einleitung; $1_5{}^a$, p. 9 Vorwort; [*rule*] C. H. Parry . . . : $1_s{}^b-33^b$, pp. 10–38 Untersuchungen; $34^a-{}^b$.

BINDING: Grey deckled cloth, rounded corners, grey end papers; lettered on front cover in a border of dots: Klassiker der Medicin Herausgegeben von Karl Sudhoff Band 10 Edward Jenner Untersuchung uber die Ursachen u. Wirkungen der Kuhpocken (1798) Verlag von Johann Ambrosius Barth in Leipzig; lettered up spine: Jenner. Ursachen und Wirkungen der Kuhpocken; at foot of spine: 10.

COPY USED: WHM.

**49A**     The same [photographic reissue]. Leipzig, Zentralantiquariat 1968.

**50**     Ispitvanje o uzrocima i posljedicama kravlje variole. [Croat translation facing English text] in Lujo Thaller, *Edward Jenner i vakcinacija velikih boginja*, Beograd, Medicinska Kniga 1949, 196 pp.

COPY: NLM.

# CHAPTER 3
# Vaccination

Perhaps some future JENNER may arise capable of discerning at one glance
the most obscure analogies, or of deducing the unknown and important
truth from a few of the simplest, but hitherto unarranged, phenomena.

Caleb Hillier Parry, *Cases of tetanus and rabies*, 1814.

Jenner considered inoculating cowpox as a preventive of smallpox for at
least ten years before he published his *Inquiry* in 1798, soon after his
forty-ninth birthday. Through the rest of his life, nearly a quarter of a
century, he campaigned continuously to promote vaccination throughout
the world. From the comparative leisure of a country surgeon, interested
in exploring problems of medicine and natural history, he took on the
busy life of a pamphleteer and a physician at Cheltenham and in London.

During these years he wrote nine books or pamphlets and many letters
to the medical journals. His increasing knowledge of vaccination made
him abandon some of the dogmatic statements in the *Inquiry*. The
writings, through which the development of his thought can be traced, are
described in this chapter in chronological order. It is confined to Jenner's
own work, not a survey of the controversies in which he became involved.

Soon after 1798 he gave up his assumption that cowpox derived from
the horse's pox-disease 'grease'. He still maintained in 1800 that vaccination gave permanent immunity, but admitted in 1801 that when smallpox
has been contracted subsequent vaccination may not stop its course. Late
in 1801 he published his 'golden rule' that vaccine fluid must be taken
between the fifth and eighth days; a truth confirmed a century later when it
was shown that virus multiplication is maximal at that period. From 1804
he advocated re-vaccination, having observed that herpes interferes with
the action of cowpox. He recognized in 1809 that 'distemper' in dogs
belongs in the group of diseases he was studying; this also was confirmed
by virologists after a century. He had great difficulty in explaining clearly
his correct concept of true and spurious cowpox, first defined in *Further
Observations* (1799) and elaborated in *The Origin* (1801), with later com-

ment in several published 'Letters'. His opponents assumed that he was deliberately excusing failures in vaccination. Baxby (1981) discussed this question in detail, recording the history of the controversy and the recent work of virologists, which has shown how complex is 'the natural history of virus infection of the bovine teat'; Baxby himself has been actively engaged in this research.

A severe epidemic of smallpox raged in England from 1816 till 1819, and doubts spread about the value of vaccination. Jenner repeatedly warned his questioners to satisfy themselves that vaccination had taken effect and, if it failed, to re-vaccinate. He reiterated this warning in a *Circular Letter*, distributed widely during 1821, which expressed his complete confidence in vaccination, when strictly carried out.

I   LETTER TO THOMAS BEDDOES

Thomas Beddoes, the Bristol physician, published a medical miscellany by various authors in 1799, which included two contributions on cowpox adverse to Jenner's inoculation proposal. Beddoes was already known in his thirties for the Pneumatic Institution, where he treated pulmonary and other disease by inhalation of oxygen and 'factitious airs', about which he had published a similar miscellany in 1795. The adverse 'Letters' were written by Charles Cooke, an apothecary at Gloucester, and Edward Thornton, a surgeon at Stroud, and printed in *Contributions to physical and medical knowledge, principally from the West of England* collected by Thomas Beddoes, M.D. Bristol: Biggs & Cottle, for T. N. Longman and O. Rees, London 1799, at pp. 387–98 and 398–402. Before publication Beddoes invited Jenner to reply; his answer was printed at pp. 468–69:

**51[44]**   Note from Dr. Jenner Respecting the preceding Facts on Cow-Pox.

'I have a pamphlet just ready for the press intended as a supplement to my former publication on the subject of cow-pox . . . A candid and judicious public will not fail to discriminate between the man who sedulously employs the greatest part of his time in making experiments for the complete investigation of a confessedly complex subject, and him who appears peremptorily to decide on the truth or falsehood of a theory . . . Edward Jenner. 26th Feb. To Dr. Beddoes'.

## II  FURTHER OBSERVATIONS

Jenner's pamphlet, 'my second treatise', appeared early in 1799 from the same printer as the *Inquiry*. The purpose of this pamphlet was 'to communicate such facts as have since occurred and to point out the fallacious sources from whence a disease resembling the true variolae vaccinae might arise'. After welcoming George Pearson's 'highly flattering confirmation', Jenner answered the criticism of Jan Ingenhousz, who asserted that smallpox had occurred after cowpox, by 'enumerating the sources of a spurious cowpox'. In particular he warned against taking the vaccine matter too late, quoting similar failures in smallpox inoculation from the experience of Charles Kite, John Earle and C. B. Trye.

The cowpox matter should be properly prepared by being 'previously dried in the open air on some compact body as a quill or a piece of glass, and afterwards secured in a small vial'.

Further reasons are given for believing in the connection between 'grease' and cowpox. Records of two new cowpox inoculations are given, and the successful resistance to smallpox inoculation of a case from the *Inquiry*.

Jenner added a footnote: 'That the cowpox was the guardian from the smallpox has been a prevalent idea for a long time past, but the similarity between one disease and the other could never have been so accurately observed had not the inoculation of the cowpox placed it in a new and stronger point of view'.

He proposed 'topical applications' of Goulard's extract of saturn (lead acetate) to check smallpox pustules. Evidence was offered of the uselessness of taking the cowpox matter too late; and Jenner gave reasons against smallpox inoculation, maintaining that it is not a complete protective. Further support for his conclusions was quoted from George Pearson, Henry Cline, William Woodville and others. Records were given of twenty inoculations made in the country by Jenner with 'London' cowpox virus. He noted that there had been 'a less disposition to erysipelatous inflammation' in patients inoculated in London. Jenner successfully inoculated cowpox in a patient suffering from measles; whereas 'it has been observed that the presence of the measles suspends the action of variolous matter'.

'The result of all my trials with the virus (of the vaccine disease) on the human subject has been uniform. In every instance the patient who has felt its influence has completely lost the susceptibility for the variolous contagion'.

*Further Observations* was re-issued by Jenner in the second edition of the *Inquiry*, with an 'Advertisement' in place of the title-page, and has been reprinted with subsequent issues. A Latin translation was published in 1799, followed by a German translation in 1800; translations were included with those of the *Inquiry* into French, Portuguese and Russian; a Japanese translation was published in 1981.

**52[45]**     Further Observations on the Variolae Vaccinae, or Cow Pox [*double rule*] By Edward Jenner, M.D. F.R.S. F.L.S. &c. [*double rule*] London: Printed, for the author, by Sampson Low, No. 7 Berwick Street, Soho: and sold by Law, Ave-Maria Lane, and Murray and Highley, Fleet Street [*ornament*] 1799.

COLLATION: 4°: A–I⁴(–A4); 3, 64 pp. 275 mm. Paper watermarked 1794.

CONTENTS: A1ᵃ Half-title; [*double rule*] Further Observations on the Variolae Vaccinae. [*double rule*] Price 2s. 6d.; A2ᵃ Title; A3ᵃ Dedication: To C. H. Parry, M.D. at Bath, 5 April 1799; B1ᵃ–I4ᵇ, pp. 1–64 Text headed Further Observations etc. etc., ends I4ᵇ, p. 64: Finis.

COPIES USED: BL, RCS, StBH, WHM (3). The BL, RCS and one of the WHM copies are separate, the others are bound with *Inquiry* 1798. StBH copy is inscribed: "To J. Abernethy Esqre. with the respectful Comts of the Author". A copy inscribed: "To H. Cline, Esqr. from his obliged friend and very humble st. the Author", was in the possession of the late Dr A. Gilpin.

**53[46]**     Eduard Jenners D.A.W.D. Fortgesetzte Beobachtungen über die Kuhpocken [*rule*] mit einigen Anmerkungen aus dem englischen übersetzt von G. F. Ballhorn D.A.W.D. [*ornamented double rule*] Hannover, in der Ritscherschen Buchhandlung. 1800.

COLLATION: 8°: A–G⁸, 112 pp. 203 mm.

CONTENTS: a1ᵃ Title; a2ᵃ⁻ᵇ Dedication; a3ᵃ–E3ᵇ, pp. 5–70 Text (begins below rule, no heading); E4ᵃ, p. 71 Half-title: Wilhelm Woodville's fortgesetzte Beobachtungen über die Kuhpocken aus dem Englischen übersetzt von G. F. Ballhorn, D.A.W.D.; E5ᵃ⁻ᵇ Dedication to Banks; E6ᵃ–G8ᵇ, pp. 75–112 Text.

COPY USED: WHM.

NOTE: Woodville's *Observations on the Cowpox* had been published early in 1800, continuing his *Report* of the previous year. Careno in the preface to his Latin translation (**38**) 1799 says that he was advised by Ballhorn, whose German translation was ready for the press, to include a translation of *Further Observations* with the *Inquiry*.

**54** Further Observations . . . [Facsimile of 1799 edition, reduced in format, preceded by Japanese translation, introduction and notes by Masao Soekawa of the Kitasato Institute] Tokyo 1981.

COLLATION: Japanese text:2 l, 79 pp, 1 l; facsimile of 1799 English edition:1 l, 64 pp; colophon 1 l; 21 cm. Dates and English names in European type within the Japanese text.

COPY USED: Dr Derrick Baxby, Liverpool, inscribed by the Editor.

III   CONTRIBUTIONS TO THE MEDICAL AND PHYSICAL JOURNAL

In January 1800 Pearson and Woodville, who were Jenner's most active advocates in London, unwittingly contaminated their cowpox matter with smallpox matter, and from the resulting variolous pustules argued that Jenner's belief in a distinct vaccine disease was illusory. Jenner pointed out the cause of their mistake in a letter to the *Medical and Physical Journal*:

**55[47]**   Dr. Jenner's Letter on the Vaccine Inoculation, *Medical and Physical Journal*, 3 (February 1800), 101–02: 'To the Editors of the Medical and Physical Journal. Gentlemen, In your Journal for the present month I observe an extract from a paper sent you by Dr. Pearson on the appearance of pustules resembling the small-pox in the vaccine inoculation . . . From the commencement of my inoculation with the vaccine virus to the present day, no pustules, similar to the variolous, have in any one instance appeared . . . I very much suspect that where *variolous pustules* have appeared, *variolous matter* has occasioned them . . . E. Jenner, Berkeley, Jan. 13, 1800.'

**56[48]**   Dr. Jenner's Answer to Mr. Shorter, *Medical and Physical Journal*, 3 (April 1800), 348–49 Shorter to the Editors, 17 February 1800; pp. 349–51 Shorter to Jenner, 25 December 1799; pp. 351–53 Jenner to

Shorter from Berkeley, 29 December 1799. Shorter recounted disappointing results with vaccine; Jenner answered his queries and objections.

One of Jenner's most active supporters, Richard Dunning of Plymouth, introduced the word 'vaccination' in his pamphlet *Some Observations on Vaccination*, London, Cadell and Davies, 1800. To elicit a further public statement from Jenner he sent questions to the *Medical and Physical Journal*, 3 (May 1800), 440–41.

Jenner answered in a letter to the Editors, written from New Bond Street, London on 15 May 1800 which was published in June:

**57[49]**     Answers to the Queries inserted in your last Journal, *Medical and Physical Journal*, 3 (June 1800), 502–03: Jenner implied that he was summarizing facts already published in his pamphlets.

IV   A CONTINUATION

Jenner's third treatise, *A Continuation of Facts and Observations*, was issued from his usual printers in the second half of 1800. It was a vindication of his conclusions against William Woodville's ambivalent evidence.

Jenner first recorded the immense mass of evidence which had accumulated in support of his conclusions, instancing in particular the work of De Carro of Vienna and Ballhorn of Hanover. As to the cases reported by Woodville, whose 'result differs essentially from mine in a point of much importance' – the variolous appearance of the pustules – 'I do suppose that [these differences] originated in the action of variolous matter which crept into the constitution in the vaccine'. Woodville's 'last report published in June' referred to very mild cases without pustules, which he attributed to the use of a very mild vaccine matter. Jenner commented; 'The decline and finally the total extinction of these pustules are more fairly attributable to the cowpox virus assimilating the variolous, the former being the original, the latter the same disease under a peculiar and at present an inexplicable modification'. He added a footnote: 'In my first publication I expressed an opinion that the cowpox and the small pox were the same diseases under different modifications . . . The axiom of the immortal Hunter that "two diseased actions cannot take place at the same time in one and the same part" will not be injured by the admission of this theory'. This is the first recognition of 'varioloid'.

Further evidence in support of cowpox inoculation was quoted from several English doctors, among them his nephews George and Henry Jenner. Some special cases were described, including cases with 'creeping scab', and another case of smallpox after smallpox inoculation.

The supposition of the temporary nature of cowpox security against smallpox is 'refuted by incontrovertible facts'.

Jenner suggests that 'the general introduction of the smallpox into Europe' by inoculation 'has been among the most conducive means in exciting' the spread of scrofula 'that formidable foe to health . . . Cowpox does not appear to have the least tendency to produce this destructive malady'.

*A Continuation* was, like *Further Observations*, repaginated and issued with the second edition of the *Inquiry* and in subsequent editions. Luigi Careno translated it into Latin in 1801 together with the *Comparative Statement*; there is a Russian translation (1896) in Vladislav Hubert's collective edition.

J. H. Marshall, who had practised at Stonehouse near Berkeley, kept a record of his vaccinations before 1800, quoted at length by Jenner in *A Continuation*. He was sent with John Walker on an official mission to the British garrisons at Gibraltar, Minorca and Malta to vaccinate soldiers, seamen and marines in October 1800. While at Malta he arranged for an Italian translation of *A Continuation* to be published. He then spent several months of 1801 in Sicily and Naples. In Paris in January 1802, during the short peace, he published a French translation of *Instructions* which was reprinted at Avignon in 1803.

**58[50]**    A Continuation of Facts and Observations Relative to the Variolae Vaccinae, or Cow Pox [*double rule*] By Edward Jenner, M.D. F.R.S. F.L.S. &c. [*double rule*] London: Printed, for the author, by Sampson Low, No. 7 Berwick Street, Soho: and sold by Law, Ave-Maria Lane, and Murray and Highley, Fleet Street [*ornament*] 1800.

COLLATION: 4°:A–E⁴, F¹; 42 pp. 261 mm. Paper watermarked 1798.

CONTENTS: A1ᵃ Half-title between double rules: A Continuation of Facts and Observations Relative to the Variolae Vaccinae; A2ᵃ Title; A3ᵃ–F1ᵇ, pp. 1–42 Text begins: A continuation of Facts and Observations &c. &c. [*double rule*] Text ends: . . . The severest Scourge of the human race. Finis. [*double rule*] Printed by Sampson Low, Berwick Street, Soho.

NOTE: A3$^b$ first paginated page 6; when reissued with *Inquiry* 2nd ed. 1800 and 3rd ed. 1801, paginated 146. On p. 31 footnote: 'See p. 55' which is also at p. 171 of the reissues. P. 36, line 2 from the bottom, and p. 37, paragraph 2, line 3: Acctati printed in error for Acetati.

COPIES USED: RCS, StBH, WHM. RCS copy inscribed: "Mr. Long with the Compliments of the Author"; StBH: "Mr. Abernethy from the Author". One of the four WHM copies has pp. 6–8 paginated 146–48, i.e. from the reissue.

**59** Continuazione di Fatti e D'Osservazioni, intorno al Vajuolo della Vacca, fatte da Odoardo Jenner, [*double rule*] Tradotto Dall'Inglese In Italiano Dall'Abate Bellet D.S. Con una Prefazione fatta dal medesimo Traduttore. [*rule*] Malta. [*rule*] 1801. 8°:32 pp.

Described with reproductions of the title-page and p. 30, part of the translator's epilogue, by Dr Paul Cassar in 'Edward Jenner and the introduction of Vaccination in Malta', *Medical History* 13 (1969), 68–70; I am indebted to Dr Cassar and to the Librarian of the National Library of Malta for information about this rare edition which appears to exist only in the three copies in the National Library at Valletta.

**60[51]** Eduardi Jenneri, Med. D. et Reg. Scient. Acad. Soc. Continuatio Disquisitionis et Observationum in Variolas Vaccinas [*ornament*] Ex Anglico in Latinum Conversa ab Aloysio Careno, M. et PhD. et Reg. Imp. Acad. Mantuanae, Societ. Patriot. Mediolanens. Reg. Taurin. Medico-Chirurg. in Helvetia, Senens. Venet. Vindobon. Monach. Matrit. Socio [*double rule*] cum Fig. colorat. [*double rule*] Vindobonae, apud Camesina. 1801.

COLLATION: 4°:χ$^6$, B–D$^4$, E$^5$; 5 l, pp. 8–41; 1 plate. 253 mm.

CONTENTS: χ1$^a$ Title; χ2$^a$–3$^b$ Praefatio . . . [signed] Careno; χ4$^{a-b}$ Lecturis (Jenner's Advertisement); χ5$^{a-b}$ [Dedication] Britann. Regi; χ6$^a$–C3$^b$, pp. [7]–22 Text; C4$^a$, p. 23 Half-title: Observationes et Facta Variolarum Vaccinarum inter se Comparata Edita a Jennero et Woodvillio . . . ; E5$^a$, p. 41 text ends.

PLATE: Nine figures printed in brown; lettered: *Pustula Vaccina Variolosa Infantilis. Cuff delin. Neidl sculp.*

COPY USED: BL.

NOTE: The plate is a re-engraving of the frontispiece of *A Comparative Statement* (1800).

# CONTINUAZIONE

DI

## FATTI E D'OSSERVAZIONI,

INTORNO AL

## VAJUOLO DELLA VACCA,

FATTE DA

# ODOARDO JENNER,

TRADOTTO DALL'INGLESE IN ITALIANO DALL'ABATE
*BELLET D. S.*
Con una Prefazione fatta dal medesimo Traduttore.

## *MALTA.*

1801.

A Continuation (Italian translation, Malta 1801)

## V   A Comparative Statement

Jenner was supported in his controversy with William Woodville by an unsigned pamphlet, issued by his own printer in a format resembling his books. Jenner's Gloucestershire friend Thomas Paytherus, now practising in London, acknowledged the authorship in the second edition; he had implicitly admitted it on page 36 of the first edition, when discussing an allegation by John Ring that cowpox virus received from Jenner through Paytherus had in one case produced variolous pustules: 'Mr. Ring has repeatedly obtained Cow-pox virus from Mr. Paytherus'. Ring had at first welcomed Jenner's discovery, but was influenced against it by Pearson; afterwards he rallied to Jenner's support.

The text consists of contrasted paragraphs from the *Inquiry* and from Woodville's *Reports* (1799) and *Observations* (1800), and passages from *A Continuation* are quoted; the coloured frontispiece is discussed below. A Latin translation was included by Luigi Careno with his Latin version of *A Continuation*, described above.

**61[52]**     A Comparative statement of facts and Observations Relative to the Cow-pox; published by Doctors Jenner and Woodville [*double rule*] Audi alteram partem [*double rule*] London: Printed and sold by Sampson Low, No. 7 Berwick Street, Soho: also sold by T. Hurst, Paternoster Row: and Mrs. Sael, Strand. Price 5s. [*ornament*] 1800.

COLLATION: $4°$:A–F$^4$(–A4), G$^2$:iv, 43 pp. 270 mm.

CONTENTS: Coloured frontispiece, lettered: *Cow Pox, Small Pox. Cuff delt. Skelton sculpt.*: A1$^a$ Half-title: A Comparative Statement of Facts and Observations; A2$^a$ Title; A3$^a$ Dedication: To Doctors Jenner and Woodville . . . by their obedient servant, The Author; B1$^a$–G2$^a$, pp. [3]–43 Text: Comparative Statement etc. etc. [*double rule*]; G2$^a$,. p. 43 . . . Finis [*double rule*] Printed by Sampson Low, no. 7 Berwick Street, Soho.

COPIES USED: BL, RCS. RCS copy inscribed "To Wm. Long, Esqr. with compliments of sincere respect" [*not in Jenner's hand*].

**62[53]**     A Comparative Statement of Facts and Observations relative to the Cow Pox [*rule*] By Thomas Paytherus, Member of the Royal College of Surgeons of London; and Fellow of the Royal Medical Society of Edinburgh [*double rule*] Audi Alteram Partem [*waved rule*] The Second

Edition [*waved rule*] London: Printed for the author, by D.N. Shury, No. 7 Berwick Street, Soho: and sold by J. Callow, Crown Court, Princes Street [*rule*] 1801.

COLLATION: 4°:A–H⁴, I²:viii, 59 pp. 257 mm.

CONTENTS: [A1ᵃ ?half-title, wanting in copy recorded]; A2ᵃ title; A3ᵃ Dedication dated January, 1801, Norfolk Street; A4, pp. [vii]–viii Advertisement; B12ᵃ–G2ᵃ, pp. 1–43 text: Comparative Statement &c. &c.: G3ᵃ–12ᵃ, pp. 45–59 A Review of the Vaccine Inoculation at Clapham.

FRONTISPIECE: Coloured plate, as in the first edition.

COPY USED: YMH (Harvey Cushing collection)

## VI   SEPARATE COW-POX ILLUSTRATIONS

The plates of cowpox pustules on the human arm published in the *Inquiry* in 1798 were engraved by William Skelton, no. 1 from his own drawing and nos. 2–4 from drawings by Edward Pearce. In the second edition they are lettered additionally *Col[oure]d by W. Cuff.* J. C. McVail claimed in 1896 that Jenner's plates represent the cowpox pustule precisely, and in 1798 showed a condition never seen before, providing direct evidence for the originality and truth of Jenner's work.

The Wellcome Institute Library owns a collection of loose copies of these prints [A] in the second edition state: fourteen copies of no. 1 (plate-mark 275 × 217 mm), thirteen of no. 2, and twelve each of nos. 3 and 4 (nos. 2–4: 270 × 210 mm); probably from Jenner's own stock of prints. With them is [B] an enlarged coloured imitation of plate 1. *W. T. Strutt sculpt.*, 236 × 135 mm. It is inscribed on the verso "Doctor Jenner", possibly in his own hand.

There are two other plates in this collection: [C] showing pustules of *Cow Pox* and *Small Pox – 3d Day* [one pustule] and the remainder in two parallel columns, *6th, 8th, 10th, 12th, 14th, 18th and 20th* days [thirteen pustules in all] *Willm Cuff del. Willm Skelton sculp.*, 274 × 214 mm, ten copies. [D] *Spurious pustule 6 Day. W. Skelton del. et sculp.*, 273 × 215 mm, eleven copies, of which only one is thus lettered, though all bear the artist's name. This illustrates the pamphlet *On the Varieties and Modifications* (1806), but was not issued with it. The pustule is shown on a right arm, similarly to the vaccine pustule on plate A2.

Wellcome Institute MS 3115 comprises thirty watercolour drawings of smallpox and cowpox inoculations by George Kirtland, copied from drawings made by Charles Gould in 1801, and used by Jenner with his Petition to the House of Commons; they were engraved and published with preliminary matter in 1802, and reproduced by McVail in 1896. A drawing of a cowpox lesion possibly given to John Hunter by Jenner in 1788 is discussed below in connection with Everard Home's evidence in favour of Jenner's claim for reward.

Another plate [E], similar to C, forms the frontispiece to Paytherus's *Comparative Statement*, described above, in both editions (*Cuff delt. Skelton sculpt.*, 225 × 138 mm). Here again the pustules of *Cow Pox* and *Small Pox* are shown in parallel columns for *8th, 10th, 12th, 18th* and *20th* days with a single figure at the bottom centre showing cowpox of *12th* day 'on the skin of an African' [nine pustules in all].

In Northcote's first portrait of Jenner (see Chapter 8, III.3) another plate [F] is shown on the table. The lettering is readable upside-down in Say's engraving of the portrait, published in 1804: *Pustules of the Cow Pox in its successive stages*, showing in two columns of five figures each a pustule for each day from 6th to 15th. I have not traced an original for this, which Northcote may have copied from a drawing. [G] Three watercolour drawings of cowpox pustules by William Cuff, the artist of C and E who also coloured A, are in the Wellcome Museum, and a drawing inscribed *Vaccine from the cow, drawn by E. Pearce*, the artist of A 2–4, is in the Crummer collection at Michigan University. Cuff gave evidence on Jenner's behalf before the House of Commons on 25 April 1802 saying that he had been employed in making the plates for illustrating Dr Jenner's system of inoculation between three and four years. George Jenner described Cuff's 'delineations and colouring' of the vaccine pustule as 'beautifully correct'.

Cuff drew an *8th Day Vaccine Pock* which was engraved by Burke on a small plate [H], 195 × 120 mm, for the *Report* of the Royal Jennerian Society for 1803. The Society's later *Reports* (e.g. 1830) contain an unsigned plate [I], 175 × 105 mm, showing *Commencement Progress and Termination of the Vaccine Pock*, with fourteen pustules.

There is no evidence to date precisely these plates, except A and E. Jenner wrote to Benjamin Waterhouse on 4 March 1801 'I have sent you one of the coloured plates which will be published with my next (fourth) pamphlet to show the progress of the perfect pustule'. The fourth pamphlet may be either *The Origin* or the *Instructions*, but no plate seems to have been issued with either; the plate sent to Waterhouse may be presumed to have been C. Waterhouse's copy of *The Origin*, now at Harvard, has, opposite the title-page, a watercolour drawing of a single vaccine pustule on a human arm, which has been reproduced by Fitz. On 30 November 1801 Waterhouse sent to John Spence of Dumfries, Virginia, 'a painting representative of the disease through all its stages sent me by Jenner. I sent one to the President [Jefferson], another to Dr Mitchill, a third to yourself and keep three for myself', which suggests prints not paintings.

Prints of plate C are bound into copies of the first and third editions of the *Inquiry* in the Harvey Cushing collection at Yale; Cushing wrote in the former: "The plate, according to George Dock, was issued (1800) in connection with the second edition of the *Inquiry* and sold with the pamphlets or separately, many being sent to the United States, where some inferior reproductions were made". The Osler Library has a copy of plate C.

A watercolour drawing corresponding closely with the engraved plate C, probably one of the 'paintings' described by Waterhouse, is at the New York Academy of Medicine. A copy of plate D, inscribed "Spurious Pustule 6th Day", was shown to me by the late Dr Richard Hunter in 1955; we agreed that the inscription was in Jenner's hand.

## VII  THE ORIGIN

On 6 May 1801 Jenner completed a short paper on *The Origin of the Vaccine Inoculation*, defending his priority. Not long afterwards he drew up a series of practical *Instructions* for vaccinators. Both were printed by D. N. Shury, who had succeeded to Low's press and issued the third edition of the *Inquiry* also during this year.

*The Origin* is of historical value in setting out Jenner's claim to have introduced cowpox inoculation; it did not directly promote the spread of his methods. He submitted it as his evidence, when petitioning Parliament.

Jenner began with the categorical statement, questioned by his adversaries, 'My inquiry commenced upwards of twenty-five years ago'. He asserted that 'the common people were very rarely inoculated for the smallpox, till the improved method introduced by the Suttons' [in the 1760s]. His own observations 'led him to form a distinction between the true and the spurious cowpox . . . I discovered the virus of cowpox was liable to undergo progressive changes . . . During the investigation of the casual cowpox I was struck with the idea that it might be practicable to propagate the disease by inoculation, first from the cow and finally from one human being to another'. This idea turned him to 'a wider field of experiment, which I went over not only with great attention but with painful solicitude'. Since the appearance of his 'treatise published in June 1798, and subsequent publications in 1799 and 1800 . . . one hundred thousand persons have been inoculated in these realms . . . It now becomes too manifest to admit of controversy, that the annihilation of the smallpox must be the final result of this practice'.

The concept of spurious cowpox arose from Jenner's recognition that there were bovine infections which, when transmitted to man, did not protect against smallpox. Jenner's observation was correct, but his exposition involved him in controversy, and led to attacks on his good faith which continued long after his death. Baxby (1981) has discussed this in detail in his Chapter 10 'True and spurious cowpox', vindicating Jenner through recent research, but commenting that 'this subject shows us Jenner both at his most brilliant and at his most evasive'.

*The Origin* was reprinted at Boston 1801 and New York 1802; a French translation with the *Instructions* appended also appeared in 1802. The text was used by Jenner in giving evidence before Parliament. J. Brendon Curgenven, a London physician, issued a quasi-facsimile in 1863. The text was included in Jones's and Crookshank's Jennerian collections and in Hubert's Russian translations.

**63[54]**     The Origin of the Vaccine Inoculation [*double rule*] By Edward Jenner, M.D. F.R.S. &c [*double rule*] London: Printed by D. N. Shury, Berwick Street, Soho. [*rule*] 1801.

COLLATION: 4°:A², B⁴:12 pp. 270 mm. Paper watermarked 1799; blue wrappers.

CONTENTS: A1ª Title; A2ª Preface without heading, below double rule: I am induced . . . Bond Street, May 6, 1801. Edward Jenner; B1ª–4ᵇ, pp. [5]–12 Text: On the origin of the vaccine inoculation; B4ᵇ colophon, below double rule: Printed by D. N. Shury, Berwick Street, Soho.

NOTE: Leaf B2 is signed, but not so in the second issue.

COPY USED: WHM inscribed on title: "W. H. Jenner, Worcester College, Oxford".

**64[55]**    The Origin . . . [Second issue, as first issue, except that leaf B2 is unsigned, and the pagination runs from B1$^b$–4$^b$ as 2–8]. Paper water-marked 1800; grey wrappers.

COPIES USED: BL, WHM. BL copy, in a volume of thirteen tracts once Lettsom's, inscribed on the title "From the Author"; of the three WHM copies: one in wrappers inscribed on the title "Mr. Pruen From the Author", one of the two bound copies has "On" added in MS, perhaps in Jenner's hand, at the beginning of the title and is inscribed "From the Author to W.D." [William Davies]; BUL from C. H. Parry's library, inscribed "From the Author", as is the Baron-Crummer copy at MiU; Harvard copy belonged to Benjamin Waterhouse; Institut de France copy presented by Jenner.

**65[55A]**    On the origin of the Vaccine Inoculation, [extracts], *London Medical Review and Magazine*, 6 (June 1801), 313–16.

**66**    On the Origin . . . , *The Columbian Centinel*, 7 November 1801 [with a preliminary note by Benjamin Waterhouse]. (John B. Blake 'An unrecorded Jenner imprint', *Journal of the History of Medicine* 9 (1954), 233–34).

**67**    On the Origin . . . in John Walker *Fragments of Letters and other Papers*, London 1802.

**68[56]**    Origin of the Vaccine Inoculation, *The Medical Repository*, New York, 5(1802), 239–42. Jenner's signed preface is included.

**69[58]**    Sur l'Origine de l'Inoculation de la Vaccine, et Instructions sur cette Pratique. Par Edward Jenner, Docteur en Médecine, Membre de la Société Royale de Londres, etc. etc. Traduit de l'Anglois. [*ornament*] Paris [*rule*] 1802.

COLLATION: 12°:A1–11:22 pp., 192 mm.

CONTENTS: A1$^a$ Half-title: Sur l'Origine de l'Inoculation de la Vaccine et Instructions sur cette Pratique; A2$^a$ Title; A3$^a$ [Preface signed] Edward Jenner. Bond-Street, 6 Mai, 1801; A4$^a$–8$^b$, pp. 7–16 text of Origin, begins below double rule: Sur l'Origine de l'Inoculation de la Vaccine; A8$^b$–11$^b$, pp. 16–22 text of Instructions, begins below double rule: Instructions Pour l'Inoculation de la Vaccine: A11$^b$, p. 22 colophon below rule: De l'Imprimerie de Bossange, Masson et Besson.

COPY USED: BL in a volume of variolation and vaccination tracts published from 1765 to 1809.

**70** Über unächten Kuhpocken, *Journal des auslandisch-medicinische Litteratur*, 1 (1802), 123–28. This article by Jenner on spurious cowpox appears to derive from *The Origin*.

**71** On the Origin . . . , in John Epps *The Life of John Walker* 1831, Appendix pp. 334–38; and in second edition 1832.

**72[57]** On the Origin of the Vaccine Inoculation [*double rule*] By Edward Jenner, M.D. F.R.S. &c. [*double rule*] London: Printed by D. N. Shury, Berwick Street, Soho. [*rule*] 1801. [*rule*] London: Reprinted by E. Elfick, 22 Leinster Terrace, W. MDCCCLXIII.

COLLATION: 4°:A$^2$, B$^4$:21, 8 pp. 248 mm.

CONTENTS: A1$^a$ Title: A1$^b$ Reprinted from an original copy in the possession of J. B. Curgenven, Esq.; A2$^a$ as 1801; B1$^a$–4$^b$, pp.[1]–8 text: On the Origin of the Vaccine Inoculation [*double rule*] My inquiry . . .; B4$^b$, p. 8 colophon as 1801. Blue wrappers, the front wrapper printed as title page.

COPIES USED: RCS, WHM. RCS copy, rebound, is inscribed: "With Mr. J. Brendon Curgenven's Compts". Inserted in WHM copy is an autograph letter from Curgenven to Frederick Mockler sending the 'reprint which about 30 years ago I had executed in as near as possible the same type and style as the original'.

**73** The Origin of the Vaccine Inoculation By Edward Jenner, M.D. F.R.S. &c. A Facsimile of the First Edition with an Introduction by Jack D. Key and Charles D. Roland. Majors Scientific Books Inc., Dallas, Texas 1977. 12 leaves: 22 cm.

1000 copies, printed on yellow paper, in stiff wrappers of dark and light brown; with reproduction of part of plate 1 from the *Inquiry* 1798.

COPY USED: Dr Derrick Baxby, Liverpool.

## VIII   Letter to William Fermor

William Fermor of Tusmore, Oxfordshire, became friendly at Cheltenham with Jenner, who afterwards visited him at his home. He found that cowpox was epizootic in his district, and published a pamphlet of *Reflections on the Cowpox*, 1800. He became an enthusiast for vaccination but, finding that inoculations sometimes failed to take, he consulted Jenner, who wrote to him on 7 September 1801 explaining his rule for securing successful vaccination.

On 11 September Fermor sent an account of the problem, with the text of Jenner's reply, to the *Medical and Physical Journal*:

**74[59]**   Dr. Jenner in Reply to Mr. Fermor, *Medical and Physical Journal* 6 (October 1801), 325–26. Fermor's letter to the Editors is at pp. 323–24.

## IX   Instructions

Baron suggests (vol. 2, p. 271) that the *Instructions* were drawn up as early as 1799, but the earliest dated reference to them as existing in print appears to be 24 February 1802 when Jenner sent a copy of 'some Rules compressed into a small space' to Waterhouse in America; this we know from the American reprint to have been Jenner's own leaflet.

In the letter to Fermor of 7 September 1801 **(74)** Jenner wrote that incessant interruptions had prevented him from publishing a fourth paper describing the best mode for inoculation. On 10 November 1801 Jenner wrote to Dr Lyman Spalding of Fairfield, New York sending 'a little paper which will perhaps furnish you with valuable intelligence. Tho' it does not come from me, it had my sanction'; J. A. Spalding, who published this letter, noted that the little paper is a statement on a single folio sheet regarding the art of vaccination. Sometime in 1801 Jenner sent one of Thomas Creaser's papers on vaccine inoculation to a correspondent (letter at RFPSG). Had his own quarto sheet of *Instructions* been ready in print Jenner would presumably have sent it. We can therefore date its appearance between November 1801 and February 1802.

Jenner's leaflet was reprinted twice in America during 1802, as a leaflet and in the *Medical Repository*. In France translations were published: an undated leaflet, in 1802 with *The Origin*, and in 1803 another leaflet. The

*Instructions* were officially reprinted for the Medical Department of the British Army in 1803 and 1806. S. B. Labatt quoted them in *An Address . . . on Vaccination*, Dublin 1840, they were reprinted by Joseph Jones in America in 1884 and 1890, and included in Hubert's Russian translations in 1896. The early American issues and the British Army reprintings reproduce Jenner's text with minor variation of paragraphing and a few omissions.

The *Instructions* describe Jenner's method of taking the vaccine fluid and of inoculating, and the proper course of appearances on the vaccinated arm. 'Vaccine virus inserted immediately is preferable, but preserving between two plates of glass is most eligible: the fluid is to be confined to a small spot about the size of a split pea, upon the centre of a glass about an inch square . . . dry in the common heat of the atmosphere, place over it a second similar glass square, and wrap it in clean writing paper. When wanted, dissolve in a small portion of cold water taken upon the point of a lancet'.

The liability of the virus to decomposition which produces the 'spurious' pustule is noted, 'the most frequent variety being that which finishes its progress much within the time limited by the true, [with] troublesome itching and premature efflorescence . . . like a common festering produced by a thorn, generally of a straw colour. The deviation arising from virus decomposed by heat shows a creeping scab of a pale brown or amber colour, making a long and slow progress, often without any perceptible efflorescence. When a 'spurious' vaccination declares itself there is a necessity of re-inoculation with vaccine virus of the most active kind, and if that is ineffectual with variolous matter. If smallpox has been contracted, the vaccine will not always stop its progress. The lancet should be perfectly clean; after each puncture, dip it into water and wipe it dry. Preservation of vaccine virus upon a lancet beyond a few days should never be attempted; as it is apt to produce rust which will decompose it'.

Jenner called the first paragraph his 'golden rule'.


**75[60]**     Instructions for Vaccine Inoculation [*double rule*] Let the vaccine fluid be taken . . . [14 paragraphs], [footnote] Edward Jenner. [*rule*] Printed by D. N. Shury, Berwick Street, Soho.

COLLATION: Folded leaf without chain marks, watermark, or signature. 24 cm.

CONTENTS: [1]ᵃ text; [1]ᵇ–[2]ᵇ blank.

COPIES USED: RCS, among John Baron's papers, dated in MS "1801"; one of the four WHM copies a single leaf: OLM a single leaf, bound with the *Inquiry* 1798 (Bibliotheca Osleriana 1264); the Jacobs copy at WML dated in Jenner's hand "1803": YMH a single leaf bound with the *Inquiry*, 3rd edition, 1801.

**76[61]**    Extract of a letter from Dr Jenner, dated London, February 24, 1802. [3 lines] Instructions for Vaccine Inoculation.

COLLATION: Folded leaf, 243 mm.

CONTENTS: 1ª Introductory note and nine text paragraphs; 1ᵇ–2ᵇ blank. No imprint.

COPIES: CLM, NYAM reproduced in my *Bio-Bibliography* (1951) plate XVIII.

Jenner's letter was to Waterhouse at Boston, where this leaflet must have been printed; a similar leaflet may have been printed at Philadelphia, but no copy is known. Dr David Ramsay of Charleston wrote on 22 July 1802 'Dr Rush has sent me a few copies of Jenner's instructions for vaccination reprinted in Philad'a. I have also got the same from Dr Waterhouse in Boston'. Ramsay's letter is in the Jacobs collection of Jenneriana at Baltimore.

**77[62]**    Instructions for Vaccine Inoculation . . . Edward Jenner. *The Medical Repository*, New York, 5 (1802) 483–85.

**78[63]**    Instructions to Regimental Surgeons, for Regulating the Concerns of the Sick, and of the Hospital. With an Appendix and Index. London: Printed by Henry Reynall, No. 21 Piccadilly, near the Black Bear. 1803.

COLLATION: sm 4°:2l, 36 pp. 18 cm; pp. 26–28 Appendix (no. V) Instructions for Vaccine Inoculation . . . Edward Jenner.

COPIES: RCS, YMH.

NOTE: The preface, leaf 2ª, is dated 'Horse Guards, September 1803' and signed 'By Order of His Royal Highness the Commander in Chief, Harry Calvert, Adjutant General'.

Reissued, with additions, in 1806. Copy: WHM.

**79**   Instructions from the Army Medical Board of Ireland to Regimental Surgeons on that Establishment . . . With an Appendix Dublin 1806.

COLLATION: 8°: 52, xlviii pages; Appendix, Section X, pp. xxiv–xxvii: Instructions . . . Edward Jenner.

COPY: RCPI.


**80[64]**   Instructions pour l'Inoculation de la Vaccine, Par Edouard Jenner. [Paris 1802?]

COLLATION: Folded leaf.

CONTENTS: [1]ᵃ blank; [1]ᵇ H. Marshall, Docteur en Médecine aux Médecins et Chirurgiens Français [rule] [Introductory note, two paragraphs]; [2]a–b Instructions.

COPY: Faculté de Médecine de Paris.


**81**   Instruction sur l'Inoculation de la Vaccine, traduit par J. H. Marshall, in J. X. B. Guerin, *Reflexions sur l'Inoculation moderne, suivies de l'Instruction de Jenner*, Avignon, F. Chambeau 1803.

COLLATION: 8°: 40 pp.

COPY: WHM.


Another French translation was included with the translation of *The Origin*, Paris 1802.


## X   Guy's Hospital Physical Society

Jenner was invited in January 1802 to the discussion at Guy's Hospital Physical Society of a paper on Variolae vaccinae which had been read on 12 December 1801 by Francis Roger Parslow, a surgical pupil of Astley Cooper. Jenner 'assisted in the debate' which continued through four weekly meetings from 9 to 30 January; in February he was elected the Society's first Honorary Associate. The Wills Library of Guy's Hospital Medical School owns a manuscript essay written on paper of 1801, almost certainly Parslow's paper, but there is no report of what Jenner said; the Library has also a first edition of Jenner's *Inquiry*, bought by the Physical Society in the year of publication, 1798. (Information from A. Baster, Assistant Librarian, The Wills Library, 1982.)

## XI  THE PETITION TO PARLIAMENT

Jenner petitioned Parliament on 17 March 1802 for recognition of his discovery of vaccination. The petition was referred to a special committee of the House of Commons which heard evidence from Jenner himself and from others and issued a report. This was debated on 2 June, and Jenner was granted £10,000.

Jenner told James Moore in 1809 that he was doubtful if his petition had been printed: 'I took care not to print it myself'. The text is summarized in the Journals of the House of Commons (vol. 57, p. 240) and seems to have been first published by R. J. Thornton in 1803.

Jenner claimed in his Petition to have discovered that cowpox admits of being inoculated on the human frame with the most perfect ease and safety, and gives security from smallpox through life; he disclosed his whole discovery and sedulously endeavoured to spread the knowledge of it; his views and wishes have been completely fulfilled; the said inoculation had already checked and must finally annihilate smallpox; his experiments have been a cause of expense and anxiety to him and interrupted the exercise of his profession; and he humbly prays for remuneration.

In 1913 Sir Ronald Ross petitioned Parliament for similar recognition of his discovery of the causative cycle of malaria. His petition was not granted, and in 1915 he published a pamphlet setting out the correspondence which he had had with the private secretary of the Chancellor of the Exchequer and other officials, and incorporating the text of Jenner's petition which he had cited as a precedent. The London School of Hygiene and Tropical Medicine possesses the correspondence about publication of this pamphlet, in the Ross Archives.

**82[65]**    Dr. Jenner's Petition. To the Honourable the Commons of the United Kingdom of Great Britain and Ireland, in Parliament assembled, Humble Petition of Edward Jenner, Doctor of Physic, in Robert Thornton *Facts decisive in favour of the Cow-Pock*, London 1803, pp. 237–40.

Thornton's book is dedicated to 'Edward Jenner, M.D., F.R.S. January 1, 1803' and contains the following Jennerian material: pp. 93–149: Sect. IX 'The discoveries of Dr. Jenner respecting the Cow-pox'; p. 235: 'Dr. Jenner's Petition and the Evidence delivered before the Honourable the Committee of the House of Commons with the Report on the same: and remuneration'; pp. 237–40: 'Dr. Jenner's Petition'; pp. 243–306: 'The Evidence'; pp. 307–15: 'Report of the . . . Committee'; p. 316: 'The Remuneration'.

**83[66]**     The humble Petition of Edward Jenner, Doctor of Physic, in John Baron *The Life of Edward Jenner*, 1 (1827), 490–91.

**84[67]**     The humble petition of Edward Jenner, Doctor of Physic, in *Correspondence concerning a petition presented to the honourable the House of Commons* by Sir Ronald Ross, K.C.B., F.R.C.S., F.R.S. *on November 8, 1913.* London and Aylesbury; Hazell, Watson and Viney, 1915, pp. 18–19.

XII   EVIDENCE BEFORE PARLIAMENT

Jenner's Petition respecting his discovery of vaccine inoculation came before a committee of the House of Commons on 22 March 1802 when he 'delivered his evidence in the form of a printed paper'; this was a copy of *The Origin* whose text was reprinted as:

**85[68]**     Dr. Jenner's Evidence, *Medical and Physical Journal*, 7 (June 1802), 489–96.

The official *Report from the Committee*, signed by Henry Bankes MP on 6 May, was printed in 1802 without the evidence they had heard. It was reprinted in the *Medical and Physical Journal*, June and July issues, and again in the House of Commons *Reports from Committees, 1793–1802*, 12 (1803), 172–88. There is a copy of the official *Report* signed by Jenner, J. C. Lettsom and S. L. Mitchill at the New York Academy of Medicine, and another signed by Lettsom in the Countway Library, Boston.

The Bodleian Library owns a German translation, *Bericht des Committee des britischen Unterhauses über die Bittschrift des Dr. Jenner*, übersetzt von Dr. C. S. Kramer, Halberstadt 1803.

Everard Home, in his evidence, recalled that Jenner had told him and other medical friends in London in 1788 about his hopes and had shown them a drawing of human cowpox. A coloured drawing of a 'cow or swine pox' lesion on a finger, in John Hunter's collection at the Royal College of Surgeons may be this drawing, which Drewy Ottley suggested was given to Hunter by Jenner in that year.

The Committee's Report was debated in the House of Commons on 2 June 1802 when Jenner was granted £10,000. George Pearson, the main opponent of Jenner's claim to reward, published an *Examination* of the Report, which was answered by Thomas Creaser's *Observations* (1803); Creaser's draft for this pamphlet, with a note in Jenner's hand, is Wellcome Institute MS 1913. Henry Hicks also published an *Answer* to Pearson in 1803.

The evidence given by and for Jenner, with an account of the debate and the opposing evidence, was edited by Jenner's nephew George in 1805; Jenner's evidence was reprinted in 1806 and 1857.

Jenner's friends laid a second claim before the House in 1806. Two drafts of his *Statement for Parliamentary friends* in the hand of Charles Murray, afterwards Secretary of the National Vaccine Institution, are in the Wellcome Institute Library (MS 3022) with a report of the debate in 1807 (MS 3023) when Jenner was awarded a further £20,000. This debate was included in Charles Murray's *Debates in Parliament respecting the Jennerian discovery including the late Debate on the further grant of twenty thousand pounds to Dr Jenner, with notes and remarks*, London, Hatchard 1808; xx, 164 pp.

**86[69]**    The Evidence at large, as laid before the Committee of the House of Commons, respecting Dr. Jenner's discovery of Vaccine Inoculation; together with the Debate which followed; and some Observations on the contravening Evidence etc. By the Rev. G. C. Jenner. Salus populi suprema lex. London: Published by J. Murray, Fleet Street, and W. Dwyer, Holborn Hill, 1805. Printed by S. Gosnell, Printer, Little Queen Street, Holborn. xxvii, 213 pp. 222 mm. Jenner's Evidence is at pp. 1–7.

COPY USED: WHM in original boards, with inscription by G. C. Jenner.

**87[70]**     Vaccinae Vindicia; or, a Vindication of the Cow-Pock. By Robert John Thornton. London, H. D. Symonds [and others] 1806; pp. 143–48 Jenner's Evidence.

**88[71]**     [Great Britain] General Board of Health. Papers relating to the history and practice of vaccination. [By John Simon.] London, George Edward Eyre and William Spottiswoode for Her Majesty's Stationery Office, 1857. 4°: 4l, lxxxiii, 188 pp.

Appendix A (pp. 1–2): Evidence given before a Committee of the House of Commons, March 22, 1802 by Dr Jenner.

### XIII   VACCINATION AT BRISTOL

Jenner encountered hostility to vaccination during a visit to Bristol because of 'accidents'. He wrote to the leading local newspaper 'such accidents attach only to the improper management of the inoculation':

**89**     Accidents in Vaccine Inoculation within the City of Bristol, Letter from Dr. Edward Jenner, *Felix Farley's Bristol Journal*, 15 May 1802.

### XIV   LETTERS TO ALEXANDER MARCET

Extracts of letters from Jenner to his friend Alexander Marcet, a prominent London physician, were published in May 1803. In the first Jenner mentioned vaccinations at Copenhagen and discussed the spurious pustule in deviations of vaccination; in the second he thanked Marcet for 'the glasses you sent me for the preservation of Vaccine matter . . . I have known the Vaccine virus in full possession of all its specific properties, when preserved in this way, seventeen weeks . . . At the expiration of three months, some Vaccine virus which I had accumulated on a quill, and suspended in a half-ounce phial, was used with complete success . . . from this virus the first patient ever inoculated in the metropolis received the Vaccine disease. It was used at my request by Mr Cline'. The autographs of both letters are at the Royal Society of Medicine.

**90[72–3]**    Correspondence between Dr. Jenner and Dr. Marcet, *Medical and Physical Journal*, 9 (May 1803), 462–66; Extract of a letter from Dr. Jenner to Dr. Marcet . . . February 23, 1803, at pp. 462–64; Extract of Dr. Jenner's Answer to Dr. Marcet . . . April 6, 1803 at p. 466.


## XV    LETTER TO LORD HARDWICKE

**91[74]**    Answer to Lord Hardwick's Letter . . . March 21, 1803, *Medical and Physical Journal*, 9 (1803), 541–42.

Lord Hardwicke, Lord Lieutenant of Ireland, had written on 18 February 1803 for guidance on vaccination, for extending the benefits to Ireland; his letter is at p. 540. The *Answer* is signed by Jenner and John Ring.


## XVI    LETTER TO G. D. YEATS

Grant David Yeats, physician to Bedford Infirmary, published *An Address to the County and Town of Bedford on the nature and efficacy of the Cow-pox, in preventing the Smallpox, with particular directions for inoculating the former; to which is annexed a letter from Dr. Jenner* Bedford [1803].


**92[75]**    Letter from Dr. Jenner 11 June 1803 on Subjects relative to the Cow-pox, in G. D. Yeats's *Address*, at pp. 53–56.

Jenner wrote that every individual who has undergone vaccine inoculation correctly is forever rescued from the contagion of the smallpox; he emphasized avoiding blunders and careful attention to inoculation. Yeats quoted another 'private letter from Dr. Jenner' on vaccination in India (p. 17), and at p. 55 recorded that he had introduced vaccine inoculation into Bedford with matter procured from Jenner.

XVII   LETTER TO LOUIS VALENTIN

Jenner wrote to Louis Valentin in Paris in 1803 asking him, according to
John Baron's account, to express in the public papers his gratitude for
many letters and printed works on vaccine inoculation from friends in
France. He promised to make up for delay in thanking foreign societies
which had sent him diplomas.

**93[76]**   [A note from Jenner], *Clef des Cabinets des Souverains*, Paris, 13
July 1803.

XVIII   LETTERS FROM JEAN DE CARRO

Jean de Carro actively promoted vaccination in the Austrian Empire and
beyond. In the autumn of 1803 Jenner published extracts from de Carro's
letters with his own notes about them, first about vaccination in Constantinople, where de Carro had introduced it with the help of Lord Elgin, the
British Ambassador, and secondly about the attempt to use vaccine as a
preventive of plague. Baron recorded that Jenner received letters about
this from many quarters, including one from Morocco forwarded by
Joseph Banks, but wrote to another friend 'I never was sanguine about
seeing plague extinguished by vaccine inoculation, as you may have seen
by the introductory to de Carro's letter in the public papers'.

**94[78]**   Edward Jenner to the public concerning cow-pox and small-pox
in Constantinople, *Bell's Weekly Messenger*, no. 394 (30 October 1803),
350–52.

**95[77]**   Vacciolous Inoculation, *Medical and Physical Journal*, 10 (November 1803), 474–75.

## XIX   VARIETIES AND MODIFICATIONS OF THE VACCINE PUSTULE

Jenner expanded the hints, which he had sent to Alexander Marcet in 1803, into an article of six pages in the August 1804 issue of the *Medical and Physical Journal*. This important statement contained his first public recognition of failures of vaccination. He also advocated re-inoculation, mentioning that he had already advocated it in his *Instructions* 'some years back'. He now wrote that herpetic affections which are evidently contagious often prevent the vaccine virus from producing its correct action, conceiving herpes to be a more frequent source of the spurious pustule than any other, or indeed, than all the rest united. He described the spurious pustule, which is to be subdued by proper applications, and the patient then re-inoculated; this point he illustrated by a case history. In another case of a child, whose face was involved in one general thick incrustation upwards of two years, the incrustation began to be less coherent, and to drop off after vaccination; and at the expiration of a fortnight the face was smooth. He attributed to herpetic state at the time of inoculation those failures where on subsequent exposure to infection, the disease [smallpox] had been taken. Jenner insisted that the vaccinator must have particular knowledge of the variolous and vaccine viruses, which often interfere with each other, and an intimate acquaintance with the character of the true and genuine vaccine pustule.

Jenner had the article reprinted as a pamphlet at Cheltenham (1806), it was reproduced by R. J. Thornton in 1806, and reissued at Philadelphia in 1818 and at Gloucester in 1819; V. O. Hubert included it among his Russian translations of Jenner's writings (1896). William Skelton's separate engraving of the spurious pustule, plate D in Section VI above, was intended to illustrate this pamphlet. The manuscript at NLM described in the *Index-Catalogue of the Surgeon-General's Library* as a draft for this, I believe to be a copy from the *Circular Letter* of 1821.

**96[79]**     Dr. Jenner, on the Effects of Cutaneous Eruptions; Dr. Jenner on Modifications of the Vaccine Vesicle [15 July 1804], *Medical and Physical Journal*, 12 (August 1804), 97–102.

**97[80]**     On the Effects . . . [as above], in R. J. Thornton *Vaccinae Vindicia*, 1806, pp. 132–40.

**98[81]**     On the Varieties and Modifications of the Vaccine Pustule, Occasioned by an Herpetic State of the Skin. [*double rule*] By Edward Jenner, M.D. L.L.D. F.R.S. &c. [*double rule*] Cheltenham, printed by H. Ruff, High Street, 1806.

COLLATION: 4°:no signatures; 13 pp. 27 cm.

CONTENTS: p. [1] Title; [3] Note signed 'E. J., Berkeley, 18th March 1806'; [5]–13 On the modifications of the vaccine pustule; 13 Text ends [*double rule*] Ruff, Printer, Cheltenham [*double rule*].

COPIES USED: RCP presented by Jenner; RCS; WHM inscribed "Mrs Kingscote with the Author's best compliments".

NOTE: There are two issues: in the second the word 'eruptions' on p. 11, line 2, is keyed by an asterisk to a footnote 'Herpetic Varieties'; YMH (Harvey Cushing copy, first issue) has this correction in Jenner's hand.

**99**     On the Varieties . . . [as above], in Jenner's *Letter to William Dillwyn*, Philadelphia 1818, described in Section XXV below.

**100[82]**     On the Varieties . . . [as 1806, reset]. Reprinted by J. Roberts, Herald Office, Gloucester. [*ornament*] 1819. Plain blue wrappers; 256 mm.

COPIES USED: BL, WHM.

## XX   LETTER TO ROBERT WILLAN

Among the many books and pamphlets written to defend vaccination, the most thorough, and in Jenner's opinion the best, was Robert Willan's. To it Jenner contributed a summary of conclusions in reference to the influence of herpes and other diseases of the skin in modifying the vaccine pustule which he had already made known in his paper of 1804.

**101[83]**     Extract of a letter from Dr. Jenner, Cheltenham, 23rd Feb., 1806, in Robert Willan *On Vaccine Inoculation*, London, 1806: Appendix I, pp. i–viii.

COPIES USED: LSH, RCS.

**102[84]**  [Jenner's Letter to Willan, German translation] in Robert Willan *Über die Kuhpockenimpfung*, aus dem Englischen übersetzt von Georg Friedrich Mühry. Göttingen, Vandenhöck, 1808.

## XXI  FACTS RESPECTING VARIOLOUS CONTAGION

Jenner returned to the defence of his proposal to revaccinate, in cases where the first vaccination failed, in the pamphlet *Facts* which he published in London at the end of 1808.

From cases published in *Further Observations* and in *A Continuation* Jenner illustrated the impossibility of total protection against the recurrence of smallpox, or its infection after inoculation. In fact after inoculation 'there is every gradation from that point in which the contagion of the smallpox excites no sensible indisposition or marks of its presence up to that which admits of the reappearance of the disease in such a degree as to prove distinctive'. He quoted two cases of smallpox *in utero* without effect on the mother; a third case was added on an inserted leaf in 1809. He reiterated that 'I now feel confident that we have a test of equal efficacy [to inoculation with variolous matter after failures of vaccination], and infinitely less hazardous, in the reinsertion of the vaccine lymph'.

Part of this pamphlet was used again by Jenner for an article on smallpox *in utero* in 1809.

**103[85]**  Facts, for the most part unobserved, or not duly noticed, respecting Variolous Contagion. [*double rule*] By Edward Jenner, M.D. L.L.D. F.R.S. &c. [*ornament*] London: Printed by S. Gosnell, Little Queen Street. 1808.

COLLATION: 4°:A–B⁴, [χ]¹:16 pp., 1 l. 248 mm.

CONTENTS: A1ᵃ Title; A2ᵃ–B4ᵃ, pp. [3]–15 Facts, [etc.] [*double rule*] . . . ; B4ᵃ, p. 15 text ends: November 18, 1808 [*rule*] S. Gosnell, Printer, Little Queen Street; [χ]1ᵃ The following case . . . has been communicated to me since the preceding pages were printed, . . . Extract of a letter from J. Kent, Esq. . . . 18th Oct., 1809 [*rule*] S. Gosnell, Printer, Little Queen Street, London. Grey wrappers.

COPIES USED: BL inscribed "Dr. Lettsom with the best regards of the Author": RCS; WHM copy 1 inscribed "Dr. Baron From the Author", in wrappers, without the 1809 leaf: copy 2 inscribed: "For Mrs. Pennant with the affectionate regards of the Author".

**104[86]**     Facts [as 1808 issue] . . . Printed by S. Gosnell, Little Queen Street, 1808. Reprinted without alteration 1811.

COLLATION: 4°:A–B⁴; 16 pp. 284 mm.

CONTENTS: A1ᵃ Title; A1ᵇ The present is a literal copy of the first edition of this Pamphlet, which was published in 1808; A2ᵃ–B4ᵃ, pp. 1–15 Text as in 1808: B4ᵃ, p. 15 colophon omitted, catch-word: The; B4ᵇ, p. 16 The following case . . . [Kent's 1809 case], colophon [*below rule*] Printed by S. Gosnell, Little Queen Street, London.

COPY USED: WHM.


XXII   DISTEMPER IN DOGS

Jenner read an account of distemper as he had observed it among Lord Berkeley's fox-hounds on 21 March 1809 to the Medico-Chirurgical Society of London, now the Royal Society of Medicine, of which he had been a founder-member in 1805. In earlier years he had satisfied himself that vaccination would prove a preventive of distemper, not because he thought the two diseases were related, but on the physiological principle of exchange, which he discussed many years later in *A Letter to C. H. Parry* (1822), where he also recalled these experiments.

On 9 December 1800 John Abernethy told the Medical and Philosophical Society of St Bartholomew's Hospital that Dr Jenner had lately been informed by a noted sportsman that inoculating dogs with cowpox matter prevented them ever afterwards having what is called the dog–distemper, of which great numbers of these animals die. This Society was renamed, after the great surgeon, the Abernethian Society. (Information from John L. Thornton.)

A news paragraph in the *Medical and Physical Journal* 6 (1801), 95 reported that Jenner had lately written to de Carro at Vienna describing his successful experiments in inoculating dogs with cowpox; and in June 1801 the King allowed Jenner and his nephew to vaccinate twenty of the royal stag-hounds. Baron recorded that many leading fox-hunters adopted the practice, but that it was soon dropped.

This paper of 1809 deals only with the clinical aspect of distemper. After stating that the contagious miasmata of distemper retain their infectious properties a long time, and that disinfection of kennels gave no good result, Jenner described the disease. 'An animal', he wrote, 'very rarely meets with a second attack' of distemper, which is not communicable to man. He quoted a case of hysterical hydrophobia described by Hunter, but he himself had never to a certainty seen a dog with hydrophobia. Later in *A Letter to C. H. Parry* (**132**) he mentioned watching and subsequently dissecting a dog with hydrophobia. 'In the distemper a dog looks dull and stupid, is always seeking after water and never satisfied with what he drinks. There can be no loss for a ready discriminating line between the two diseases.'

The isolation of the distemper virus and the production of anti-distemper vaccine was not achieved until the 1930s.

**105[87]**    Observations on the Distemper in Dogs. By Edward Jenner M.D. F.R.S. Read March 21, 1809, *Medico-chirurgical Transactions* 1(1809), 263–68: reprinted in second edition 1812, and third edition 1815.

**106**    Observations on the Distemper in Dogs, *Eclectic Repertory and Analytical Review*, edited by a Society of Physicians, Philadelphia, 1 (1811), 1–4.

**107[88]**    Observations . . . [French translation], *Transactions médico-chirurgicales*, traduites par J. L. Deschamps, Paris 1811.

**108[89]**    Beobachtungen über eine Krankheit bei Hunden, *Medicinisch-chirurgische Abhandlungen*, übersetzt von Emil Osann, Berlin 1811.

XXIII    SMALLPOX *IN UTERO*

At a subsequent meeting of the Medico-Chirurgical Society on 4 April 1809 Jenner recounted two case histories of smallpox infection of the foetus before birth, communicated through the mother, herself being already secure from any visible occurrence of the disorder. These had already been published in his pamphlet *Facts*; this article quoted the relevant passages verbatim from pp. 12–15; it is dated 18 November 1808, as was *Facts*. In addition to the two case histories the first and last paragraphs are quoted from *Facts* and there are four new paragraphs on pp. 270–71 of this article.

**109[90]**    Two Cases of Small-pox Infection, communicated to the Foetus in utero under peculiar Circumstances: with additional remarks. Read April 4, 1809, *Medico-chirurgical Transactions*, 1 (1809) 269–75; reprinted, as was no. 105, in second and third editions, 1812 and 1815.

**110**    Two cases . . . as **106**, in *Eclectic Repertory* . . . , Philadelphia, 1 (1811), 4–8.

**111[91]**    French translation, as **107**.

**112[92]**    German translation, as **108**.

'Distemper in Dogs' and 'Smallpox in Utero' were abstracted with comments in *Medical and Physical Journal*, 22 (1809) 240–43.

## XXIV    Answers to James Taylor

James Taylor in a letter to the Editor of the *Gentleman's Magazine* from Millman Place, dated 24 November 1810, reported answers which he had received from Jenner to three questions about vaccination: (1) Jenner had held no post under the College of Physicians; he was nominated Director of the National Vaccine Institute, but did not accept; (2) he did not inoculate his son with variolous matter in preference to vaccination; (3) his present opinions of vaccination were precisely the same as before.

**113[93]**    [Letter from James Taylor, quoting letter from Edward Jenner], *Gentleman's Magazine*, 80 (December 1810), 523–24.

## XXV  Letter to William Dillwyn

Jenner wrote to an American friend, William Dillwyn, to dispel his doubts about the efficacy of vaccination in 1818, the year of the first severe smallpox epidemic since vaccination began. Dillwyn, who was living at Walthamstow near London, caused the letter to be published at Philadelphia, his home city, with documents which Jenner had sent him; reports on vaccination in Sweden and Spain; and the text of Jenner's *Varieties and Modifications*. Jenner's letter quoted from S. B. Labatt's annual reports of the Dublin Cow-pock Institution on the success of vaccination in Ireland, and concluded *My confidence of the efficacy of the Vaccine, to guard the constitution from the small pox, is not in the least diminished* [italics in the printed text].

**114[94]**    Letter from Doctor Edward Jenner, to William Dillwyn, Esq., on the effects of vaccination, in Preserving from the Small-Pox. To which are added sundry documents relating to vaccination, referred to and accompanying the letter. [*double rule*] Published by the Philadelphia Vaccine Society. William Fry, Printer. 1818.

COLLATION: 4°:A–B⁴, C²; 20 pp. 214 mm.

CONTENTS: A1ᵃ Title; A1ᵇ Introduction; A2ᵃ–3ᵇ, pp. [3]–6 Letter to Wm Dillwyn, Esq., Higham Lodge, Walthamstow, Essex . . . Edw. Jenner, Berkeley, Glostershire, 19th August, 1818; A4ᵃ–B2ᵃ pp. 7–11 Appendix I, Copy of a Letter from the President of the National Vaccine Establishment to Lord Sidmouth, dated July 15, 1814, enclosing Report on the State of Vaccination in Sweden, February 10, 1814; B2ᵇ–4ᵃ pp. 12–15 Appendix II, Supplement to the Madrid Gazette of October 14, 1806; B4ᵇ–C2ᵇ pp. 16–20 Appendix III, To the Editors of the Medical and Physical Journal. [Letter signed] Edward Jenner, Berkeley, July 15, 1804 [i.e. Varieties and Modifications of the Vaccine Pustule].

COPY USED: BL.

The text of Appendix II had been issued as a leaflet: Supplement to The Madrid Gazette of the 14th October, 1806. Ruff, Printer, Cheltenham [1806] 8°: 4 pp.

COPIES USED: BL bound with *Facts*; RCS among Baron's papers; NYAM with a covering note from Jenner dated Decr. 21, 1806 and a copy (**114A**) of the Spanish original: Suplemento a la Gazeta de Madrid del Martes 14 de Octubre de 1806 (En la Imprenta real; 2 leaves). The English version was made for Jenner by Lord Lansdowne.

# SUPLEMENTO

## A LA GAZETA DE MADRID

DEL MARTES 14 DE OCTUBRE DE 1806.

El domingo 7 de Setiembre próximo pasado tuvo la honra de besar la mano al Rey nuestro Señor el Dr. D. Francisco Xavier de Balmis, Cirujano honorario de su Real Cámara, que acaba de dar la vuelta al mundo con el único objeto de llevar á todos los dominios ultramarinos de la Monarquía Española, y á los de otras diversas Naciones, el inestimable don de la Vacuna. S. M. se ha informado con el mas vivo interes de los principales sucesos de la expedicion, mostrándose sumamente complacido de que las resultas hayan excedido las esperanzas que se concibiéron al emprenderla.

Esta expedicion, compuesta de varios Facultativos y empleados, y de veinte y dos niños, que no habian pasado viruelas, destinados á conservar el precioso fluido, transmitiéndolo sucesivamente de brazo á brazo, y de unos á otros en el curso de la navegacion, salió del puerto de la Coruña baxo la direccion de Balmis en 30 de Noviembre de 1803: hizo su primera escala en Canarias, la segunda en Puerto-Rico, y la tercera en Caracas. Al salir de esta provincia por el puerto de la Guayra se dividió en dos ramos, navegando el uno para la América Meridional al cargo del Subdirector D. Francisco Salvani; y dirigiéndose el otro con el Director Balmis á la Havana, y de allí á Yucatán. En esta provincia se subdividió, saliendo el profesor D. Francisco Pastor del puerto de Sisal para el de Villahermosa en la provincia de Tabasco á propagar la Vacuna por Ciudad Real de Chiapa hasta Goatemala, dando la vuelta por el dilatado y fragoso camino de quatrocientas leguas hasta Oaxaca, miéntras que el resto de la expedicion, que arribó felizmente á Veracruz, no solo recorria todo el Vireynato de Nueva Espana, sino las Provincias internas, de donde debia regresar á México, que era el punto de reunion.

Prodigado ya por toda la América Septentrional hasta las

Suplemento (Madrid 1806)

88

## XXVI  John Fosbroke's Remarks

John Fosbroke, writing in the *London Medical Repository* for June 1819, included some notes on 'secondary smallpox' [varioloid] sent to him by Jenner, with further information from Jenner referring to J. H. Hickes's unpublished account of the mild epidemic of smallpox in Gloucestershire in 1791, mentioned at p. 54 of the *Inquiry*. John Thomson, who was quoted by Fosbroke, introduced the word 'varioloid' in his paper 'Some observations on the Varioloid disease', *Edinburgh Medical and Surgical Journal*, 14 (October 1818), 518.

**115[95]**     Some remarks upon the late epidemic eruptive diseases supervening on variola and vaccinia, and upon Professor Thomson's theory of the identity of modified smallpox and chickpox; with some contributions to diagnosis, by J. Fosbrooke [sic], *London Medical Repository*, 11 (April 1819), 265–77 and (June 1819), 463–76. At pp. 465–66, 'Dr. Jenner has personally favoured me with some ingenious and original additions [including] anecdotes of secondary small-pox' [Jenner's words are quoted at length]; at p. 470 Jenner's information about Hickes's unpublished account of the epidemic of 1791; at p. 472–75 further quotations from Jenner.

## XXVII  The Circular Letter

During the great epidemic of 1816–19, which was most severe in 1818, smallpox spread to many who had previously been inoculated with smallpox or cowpox. Jenner believed that improper vaccination was the main cause of these apparent re-infections. He assumed, correctly, that the failure of inoculated cowpox to take its proper course was frequently overlooked, and decided that the warning which he had reiterated since 1804 must be made generally known.

He printed a circular letter in January 1821 pointing out this fact, and asking professional colleagues for information about their experience. He sent out copies of this letter, often with written additions in his own hand, and he had its text inserted in the medical journals and the lay press. It was reprinted at Philadelphia, and published in German at Berlin. The *Circular Letter* is partly questionnaire and partly advice. Jenner 'takes the liberty of requesting to be informed:

*67483*

*Berkeley*
*August 30*
*1821*

*Dear Madam*

PRESUMING that you are conversant with the practice of Vaccine Inoculation according to the instructions which I have formerly published, and that you may have seen, in addition to my general observations, those which I have since made and promulgated, respecting the "Varieties and Modifications of the Vaccine Pustule, occasioned by an herpetic and other eruptive states of the skin," I take the liberty of requesting to be informed, whether the observations acquired in your own practice coincide with mine? That is to say, whether the Vaccine Vesicles, under these contingent circumstances, go through their course with the same regularity as when the skin is free from diseases of this description?

*Secondly,* Whether, on the other hand, such individuals are more liable to resist the legitimate action of Vaccine Lymph when inserted into the arms, than those who are free from such eruptive affections?

*Thirdly,* Whether you have met with cases of Small-Pox, or what has been termed the Varioloid Disease, after Vaccination ; and if so, whether in such cases you ascertained those deviations at the time of Vaccination in the progress of the pustules on the arms, which I have described as liable to take place when the skin is affected with herpetic and other eruptions?

As you may not have the paper before you, to which I here allude, nor the short series which followed it, I will point out the periods of their publication, and where they are to be found. The first was published in the Medical and Physical Journal, No. 66, for August 1804, and gives an outline of the subject, of some extent. It points out the fact, that a single serous blotch upon the skin, existing during the progress of the Vaccine Vesicles on the arms, may occasion such irregularity and deviation from correctness, that Vaccination under such circumstances cannot be perfectly depended on.

I have found abrasions of the cuticle to produce the same effect ; such for example as we find in the nurseries of the opulent, as well as the cottages of the poor, behind the ears, and upon many other parts where the cuticle is thin. Happily we find no irregularity in the Vaccine Vesicle in an uncontaminated skin ; but we find it if the skin is beset with these herpetic blotches, or even simple serous oozings from an abraded cuticle. It is not to be considered as of less consequence when occupying a small space ; a speck behind the ear which might be covered by a split pea, being capable of disordering the progress of the Vaccine Vesicle. Dandriffe may be considered as a malady of this class, the incrustation on the scalp being formed from excoriation beneath ; and however slight, for there is every gradation between a thin scurfy layer of a dirt-looking substance, or even patches of this thin crust, and Tinea itself. However, fortunately for the safety of the Vaccine Practice, and fortunately too for the ease of the practitioner, all these affections of the skin may be removed with very little trouble.* Sore eyelids are also impediments to constitutional Vaccination.

The second paper relating to this subject was given by the late Dr. Willan, in answer to the following interrogatory, addressed to me by himself:† " What are the changes produced in the vesicle, when a person is affected during Vaccination with the Shingles, the Vesicular Ringworm, or Impetigo?"

To this question I made a full, and, I believe, a satisfactory reply. Its purport will be shewn by quoting a few sentences from it. " To answer this question in its fullest extent, would lead me through a wide field of observation, which I mean to go over at a future time ; but the following answer may probably convey to you as much information upon the subject as you may now require." " Vaccination, under the circumstances you mention, usually produces a striking deviation from the perfect character of the Vaccine vesicle at some period or other of its

---

* The most effectual application which I know for subduing these cuticular diseases, that produce impediment, is the Unguentum Hydrargyri Nitratis, as much lowered with Unguentum Cetacei, or any other bland ointment, as the irritability of the subject may require. The Dandriffe demands a double process—the *first* consists in removing the incrustation, the *second* in subduing the oozing. There are skins that will not well bear unctuous applications : the desiccative lotions may then be made use of two or three times a-day ; such as those prepared with the sulphate of zinc or superacetate of lead, &c.
† It was published in the year 1806, in his Treatise on Vaccine Inoculation.

Circular Letter (1821)

(1) Whether the vaccine vesicles, under contingent circumstances of herpetic or other eruptive states of the skin, go through their course with the same regularity as when the skin is free from diseases of this description?

(2) Whether individuals [with herpetic diseases] are more liable to resist the legitimate action of the vaccine lymph?

(3) Whether you have met with cases of smallpox, or the varioloid disease, after vaccination?'

Jenner recalled his *Varieties and Modifications of the Vaccine Pustule* (1804) and his published *Letter to Robert Willan* (1806), which 'comprehend, first, the simple fact of important deviations being produced by diseases in pre-occupation of the skin; and, secondly, a general account of the character of these deviations, and their differing degrees of influence upon the vaccine protection'. He referred also to observations published by Alexander Wilson Philip of Worcester in his *Treatise on Febrile Diseases* [third and fourth editions, 1813 and 1820], where Philip mentioned Jenner's opinions with approval (*Bio-Bibliography* (1951), **105** (but not in Jenner's own words)).

**116[96]**      [Circular Letter.] No title, heading, or imprint [January 1821?].

COLLATION: 4°:2l., 253 mm.

CONTENTS: Leaf 1 pp. [1]–2 Text; leaf 2 blank.

TEXT BEGINS: Presuming that you are conversant with the practice of Vaccine Inoculation . . . ; *ends:* . . . or producing a new action by external violence. I have the honour to be, Yours, etc. [Two footnotes on each page].

COPIES USED: BmMI, WHM (2).

NOTE ON COPIES: BmMI has on the back ALS of 9 February 1821 from Jenner at Berkeley to "Jas. White Esq., Vetr. Surgeon, Bath"; WHM (copy 1) completed in Jenner's hand, at top of p. 1: "Circular. Berkeley: Jan. 31, 1821. Dear Pruen"; at foot of p. 2: "Dear Pruen very truly Edw. Jenner"; addressed across p. 4: "To the Rev. T. Pruen, Rectory, Dursley"; WHM (copy 2) signed and dated August 3, 1821, with an autograph letter to Miss Cox, Painswick.

**116A[96a]**    Variant: text lacks formal ending 'I have the honour to be Yours, etc'.

COPIES: EUL with MS notes by John Fosbroke; MiU (John Baron – Leroy Crummer volume) completed in Jenner's hand: at top of p. 1 "Berkeley, July 25, 1821". "Dear Sir", and on pp. [3–4] AL in third person from Dr. Jenner, for "Dr. Walshman, Carrington Row"; RCP with Jenner's autograph additions, to "The Rev. Robert Ferryman, January 23, 1823" (three days before Jenner died), presented by Brigadier E. Mockler Ferryman in 1951.

**117[98]**    [Circular Letter], *Gloucester Journal*, 12 January 1821.

**118**    [Circular Letter], *Cheltenham Chronicle*, 12 January 1821.

Baron's reference to a Devizes issue (*Bio-Bibliography* 1951, **97**) seems an error for:

**119**    Vaccination. The following letter on this interesting subject has been addressed by the celebrated Dr. Jenner to a lady resident near Devizes . . . [signed] Edward Jenner. Berkeley. Jan. 11, 1821, *Cheltenham Chronicle*, 16 January 1821.

**120**    –Reprinted: *New Monthly Magazine*, 3 (1 March 1821), Historical Register p. 111.

**121**    –Reprinted: Paul Saunders *Edward Jenner* 1982, pp. 415–16.

**122[99]**    Dr. Jenner's Circular Letter to the Profession . . . Berkeley, January 28, 1821. *Medico-chirurgical Review and Journal of Medical Science*, 1 (March 1821), 780–88.

**123[100]**    Letter addressed to the Medical Profession generally, relative to vaccination. By Dr. Edward Jenner . . . Berkeley, February 1821, *London Medical and Physical Journal*, 45 (April 1821), 277–80.

**124[101]** Vaccination. Dr. Jenner's Circular to the Medical Profession, pointing out the causes of those affections which have occasionally followed Vaccinia and Variola, known by the term Varioloids. Communicated under the author's authority by John Fosbroke, Esq., *Edinburgh Medical and Surgical Journal*, 17 (1 July 1821), 476–78.

NLM possesses a manuscript copy of this issue in an unknown hand, inserted in a copy of the *Inquiry* 1798.

**125[102]** [Circular Letter], *London Monthly Magazine*, November 1821.

**126[103]** [Circular Letter], *National Gazette and Literary Register*, Philadelphia, 26 December 1821.

**127[104]** Dr. Jenner's Rundschreiben an die Aerzte in Betreff der Ursachen der unter dem Namen der falschen Pocken (Varioloids) bekannten Ausschläge, die zuweilen auf Schutz- und Menschenpocken gefolgt sind. Im Namen des Verfassers von John Fosbroke, Esq. mitgeteilt. Aus dem Edinburgh medical and physical Journal, Julius 1821, *Journal der practischen Arzneykunde und Wundarzneykunst* herausgegeben von C. W. Hufeland, Berlin, G. Reimer, Band 54, *Neues Journal*, Band 47, (Januar 1822), 64–71.

Hufeland wrote in a footnote 'every doctor will rejoice to hear the Father of Vaccination, the immortal Jenner, express his latest views'.

XXVIII    LETTER TO GEORGE GREGORY

George Gregory, physician to the Smallpox and Vaccination Hospital, London, answered Jenner's *Circular Letter* on 22 June 1821 asking him in return ten questions about vaccination; Jenner answered from Berkeley on 31 July. Gregory sent the correspondence to the *London Medical and Physical Journal*, where it was printed in September 1822.

Jenner asserted (1) strict attention to vaccinating will produce complete protection; (2) no other impediments to vaccination than those named in the *Circular Letter* are at present known to him; (3) as to revaccination, imperfect vesicles are open to a second action in different gradations; (4) failure of revaccination is decisive in favour of the first process; (5) after imperfect vaccination, varioloids in all their gradations may occur, but it is impossible always to procure the requisite information about secondary infection; (6) his confidence in the power of vaccination to exterminate smallpox altogether has increased in the highest degree, his statements about its success abroad being based on authentic private and public sources.

**128[106]**    A Letter to the Editors, from George Gregory, M.D., Physician to the Smallpox and Vaccination Hospital; inclosing a Correspondence with Dr Jenner on the Subject of Smallpox after Vaccination, *London Medical and Physical Journal*, 48 (September 1822), pp. 191–92 letter from Gregory to Jenner 22 June 1821, pp. 193–95 letter from Jenner to Gregory 31 July 1821.

# CHAPTER 4
# Medical Digressions

Jenner's pamphlet is more like a letter from an intelligent squire, than a scientific treatise.

H. H. Bashford *The Harley Street Calendar* 1929, on *An Inquiry*.


### I  CLASSES OF THE HUMAN INTELLECT

In the summer of 1807, while waiting for Parliament's decision on his second claim for financial reward, Jenner wrote a slight essay in psychology for his friend Prince Hoare. It appeared in Hoare's weekly journal *The Artist*. Prince Hoare, painter and writer, was a seasonal visitor to Cheltenham and had written a comedy about it; he was foreign secretary of the Royal Academy, and had many prominent friends besides Jenner. This classification of the 'varieties of intellect' is not a serious contribution to knowledge, yet Jenner reprinted it in 1820. The article has no heading, and I use the title in the list of contents of the magazine; it is signed 'E.J.'.

Jenner proposed a sevenfold classification: (1) The Idiot: the mere vegetative being. (2) The Dolt: the weak, silly, poor creature. (3) Mediocrity: the large mass of mankind. (4) Mental Perfection: from this point intellect again diverges. (5) Eccentricity: 'I have in this class a very numerous acquaintance'. (6) Insanity: the most affecting of all conditions, illustrated from the life of William Cowper, whose verses are quoted. (7) The Maniac: the wreck of the mental faculties.


**129[107]**    Classes of the Human Powers of Intellect – Hints for a Classification of the Powers of the Human Mind as they appear in various Descriptions of Men – Examples of Excellence rare – General Division into seven Classes – Difficulty of analysing all the Varieties of Intellect in Individuals. By Dr. Jenner. *The Artist; a collection of essays, relative to*

95

*painting, poetry, sculpture, architecture, the drama, discoveries of science, and various other subjects*, edited by Prince Hoare. London, 1, no. xix, (18 July 1807), 1–7.

*The Artist* was published by John Murray, in parts independently paged, from 14 March 1807 till 1809.

**130[108]**     [Classes of Intellect] Pamphlet without title page [1820].

COLLATION: 7 pp., 265 mm.

CONTENTS: as London issue; p. 7 colophon: S. V. Griffith, Printer, Chronicle Office, Cheltenham.

COPIES: MiU (Crummer collection in Baron's volume), ViU.

NOTE: The layout follows the London original closely; Jenner allowed S. V. Griffith, in financial difficulties in 1820, to reprint this essay (Saunders, 1982, p. 408).

## II   A LETTER TO CHARLES HENRY PARRY

Jenner's last book, addressed to the son of his old friend Caleb Hillier Parry, now a paralysed, dying man, summarized the observations of a lifetime on counter-irritation by means of emetic tartar ointment, and discussed the physiological principles on which the application acts. He wrote that his references went back to 1794, the year after his recipe for emetic tartar had been published, though that paper had been written ten years earlier still. In this *Letter to Parry* Jenner also referred to the 'interesting observations' of Thomas Bradley in the *Memoirs of the Medical Society of London* for 1773. His interest in the subject thus appears to go back to the very start of his medical career, while the evidence which he adduced is from the most recent years 1819–21. Most of Jenner's evidence is from cases to which he had been called in consultation, and he published other cases reported to him by Fewster of Thornbury, Fry of Dursley, John Fosbroke, and his nephew George Jenner, friends whose names recur in his medical life. The text is dated November 1821.

At Edinburgh University Library there is a proof copy:

**131[109a]**    A letter to Charles Henry Parry [as published] By Edward
Jenner M.D. F.R.S. &c. &c. &c. [*rule*] London: Printed by John Nichols
and Son, Parliament Street. [*rule*] 1821.

COLLATION: 4°:A–H⁴; 61 pp. 243 mm.

CONTENTS: A1ᵃ Title; A2ᵃ–H3ᵃ, p. [3]–61 text; H3ᵇ–4ᵇ blank.

NOTE: The title-page is inscribed 'for Mr. J. Fosbroke' who was Jenner's assistant at
this time. There are a number of manuscript corrections through the text, which
were not all used; a summary of cases on pp. 23–25 of the proof was omitted, while
the letter from George Jenner, pp. 61–64 of the published book, is not in the proof;
the text of pp. 65–67 of the book is expanded from a ten-line manuscript draft on
p. 61 of the proof.

Jenner wrote in an undated letter to Edward Davies 'I want much to see
you on account of *the Book* – the copies (500) are all printed off by a hasty
mistake of Fosbroke; but 'tis well the work is not published, for much of it
must be new modell'd . . . I am very unhappy about the Book and fear the
whole must be cancell'd, for a slice off one's purse is as nothing compared
to a shaving taken from one's reputation'. He repeated this phrase in a
letter of 5 December 1821, and wrote to the printer about the book on 1
January 1822. He had written to Charles Parry, 27 December: 'Your
printed book made its escape, but I had the good fortune to recommit it,
. . . it underwent a thorough reform'.

Jenner postulated a sympathy between the constitution and the skin, in
all probability through the brain and nervous system, which would
account for the constitutional effects of eruptive diseases. He suggested
that new cuticular diseases may be helpful in treating not only non-
exanthematous diseases but in certain diseases generated by animal
poisons: 'I have long considered tetanus as one of the diseases which owes
its origin like hydrophobia to a morbid poison'. He reminded Parry that he
had long ago hinted that the febrile attack of the cowpox might afford
relief from various non-eruptive diseases, upon well-known physiological
principles.

In connection with infections of the sinuses, he recalled his experiments
in inoculating dogs with cowpox against distemper and mentioned 'staggers' in horses. 'Typhus, yellow-fever and rheumatism might be com-
prised within the sphere of our experimental attempts . . . I suspect that
dysentery in the first instance is an affection of the brain'.

The cases, whose treatment by counter-irritation is recorded, comprise hysteria or mania (five), depressive insanity (four), senile insanity and chorea (one each), pulmonary affections (five), and digestive diseases (two). To be successful, a secreted fluid must appear in the vesicles which are induced; for the treatment works by exchanges of diseased action.

Two *obiter dicta* from this book may be quoted, characteristic of Jenner's manner of thought and writing: 'Muscular exertion, which tends to equalize the circulation, may be involuntarily called into violent action, for distributing a preternatural quantity of blood thrown upon the brain during the paroxysms, and which, if impeded, would be followed by consequences injurious to the structure . . . I would just notice not only those *involuntary* and sudden motions which we designate by the term "fits", whether epileptic, hysteric, or whatever they may be, but also the *voluntary* motions, when the brain has become turgid from any adequate exciting cause, produced under various modifications of vehemence, from the thump on the cushion to the contortions of the orator, as so frequently exhibited within the walls of the Houses of Parliament. How well do I remember the strong and characteristic action of the late Messrs Fox, Pitt, Grattan and a host of public characters . . . It is to be lamented that the opulent in most countries pay so little attention to these abodes of wretchedness [parish workhouses]. When sickness and poverty unite, no uncommon union here, let those who have felt the *one* (and who has not felt it?) conceive, if they can, the situation when united with the *other*'.

The *Letter to Parry* was reprinted in America, and translated into Dutch and French.


**132[109]**    A Letter to Charles Henry Parry, M.D. F.R.S. &c. &c. on the Influence of Artificial Eruptions, In certain Diseases incidental to the Human Body, with an Inquiry respecting the probable advantages to be derived from further Experiments [*rule*] By Edward Jenner, Esq., M.D. LL.D. F.R.S. M.N.I.F. &c. &c. &c. and Physician Extraordinary to the King [*rule*] London: Printed for Baldwin, Cradock, and Joy, Paternoster Row. [*rule*] 1822.

COLLATION: 4°:(A)–H⁴, I²; 67 pp. 278 mm.

CONTENTS: A1ᵃ Title; A1ᵇ London: Printed by J. Nichols and Son, 25 Parliament Street; A2ᵃ–I2ᵃ, pp. [3]–67 Text begins: A letter to Charles Henry Parry, M.D. F.R.S. &c. &c. on the influence of artificial eruptions. [*rule*] My Dear Charles, In our conversations . . . [ends] My dear Charles, with best wishes, Your faithful friend and servant, Edward Jenner. Berkeley, Nov. 1821; I2ª colophon: John Nichols and Son, Printers, 25 Parliament Street, Westminster.

COPIES USED: BL, RCS, WHM.

INSCRIBED COPIES: BUL: "Phil. Hicks Esqr. From the Author"; University of Western Ontario: "to Richard Smith" [a Bristol surgeon]; WHM (1): "Mr. H. Jenner from the Author"; (2): "Mr. Hands from the Author"; (3): "The Rev. T. Pruen From the Author"; Crummer copy: "Dr. Baron with best regards from the Author".

**133[110]**    A Letter to Charles Henry Parry, M.D. F.R.S. &c. &c. on the Influence of Artificial Eruptions, in certain Diseases incidental to the Human Body, with an Inquiry respecting the probable advantages to be derived from further Experiments, *The American Medical Recorder*, Philadelphia, 5 (October 1822) 684–725.

RUNNING TITLE: Dr. Jenner on Artificial Eruptions.

**134**    Letter to Parry, *Monthly Journal of Medicine*, Hartford, Connecticut, 1 (January 1823) 3–24.

**135[111]**    Over den invloed van den door Kunst voortgebragten Uitslag, in zekere Ziekten; Benevens een Onderzoek nopens het waarschijnlijke Nut, dat men van verdere proeven mag verwachten.
   In eenen Brief van Edward Jenner, buitengewoon geneesheer van den koning van Engeland, lid van verscheidene genootschappen, enz. aan C. H. Parry, M.D. F.R.S. etc. Uit het Engelsch. [*ornament*] Te Rotterdam, bij J. Hendriksen, 1822.

COLLATION: 8°:[χ]⁴, A⁶, B–D⁸, E⁶; vi, 76 pp. 232 mm.

CONTENTS: [χ]1ª Title; [χ]2ª–4ᵇ, p. [i]–vi Voorberigt [*signed*] J. Gijsberti Hodenpijl, Medicinae Doctor. Rotterdam den 21 Nov. 1822; A1ª–E6ᵇ, pp. 1–76 text. Grey-blue covers: half-title on front cover, within decorative border: [*rule*] E. Jenner de door Kunst voortgebragten Uitlsag [sic].

COPY USED: YMH, Harvey Cushing's copy, untrimmed with the original covers bound in.

**136** Lettre à Charles-Henri Parry M.D., Sur l'Influence des Éruptions artificielles dans certaines Maladies; Avec une recherche relative aux avantages probables qui peuvent résulter d'expériences faites ultérieurement. Par Édouard Jenner, Écuyer M.D. etc. etc.; et médecin extraordinaire du Roi. Londres, 1822. Traduction faite de l'Anglais Par A. F. T. Jouenne, M.D., Des facultés de Caen et de Louvain; Membre de plusieurs sociétés savantes. [rule] A Bruxelles, chez H. Remy, Rue de l'Empereur, No. 812 [rule] 1822.

COLLATION: 8°: [χ]², 1–5⁸, 6⁶; 96 pp. 212 mm.

CONTENTS: [χ]1 Title; [χ]2 Dedication to "Professeurs Curtet et Baud"; 1₁a–4b, pp. [5] – 12 Advertisement; 1₅a–6₆b text.

COPY USED: RCS, acquired from Dawsons, booksellers 1955.


**137[112]** De l'Influence des Éruptions Artificielles dans Certaines Maladies, par E. Jenner, Auteur de la Découverte de la Vaccine, etc.; Traduit de l'Anglais par J . . . des Facultés de Caen, de Louvain, etc. [ornament] Paris, Roret, Libraire, rue Hautefeuille, au Coin de Celle du Battoir [rule] 1824.

COLLATION: As Brussels edition. 199 mm.

CONTENTS: [χ]1ᵃ Half-title: De l'Influence des Eruptions Artificielles; [χ]2ᵃ Title; [χ]2ᵇ J.-M. Eberhart; 1₁a–4b, pp. 5–12 Advertisement du Traducteur; 1₅a–6₆b, pp. 13–96 text.

COPY USED: MML from the Manchester Medical Society, bound in a volume of five French tracts including Valentin's *Notice sur Jenner*, second edition 1824.

## CHAPTER 5

# Posthumous Works

I love to be puzzled, for then I am sure I shall learn something valuable.

John Hunter: Spoken to Benjamin Waterhouse, and recorded by him in a letter to Jenner, 24 April 1801.

## I MIGRATION OF BIRDS

Jenner's paper on bird migration was read to the Royal Society six months after his death. It had been written many years earlier, and is the first contribution of value towards the explanation of a phenomenon now well known in great detail, though not fully elucidated. When it was written migration was still doubted; Jenner easily established the fact, but the purpose of his paper was to determine the cause. He was the first to demonstrate that the prime cause of migration is 'to produce an offspring'.

Jenner's manuscript is not now known, but his references in the paper published in 1824 to eighteenth-century naturalists, Gilbert White, Thomas Pennant and John Hunter, whom he called 'my late valued friend and honoured preceptor', suggest that it belongs in the main to the years immediately after Hunter's death.

In the winter of 1794–95 when Jenner was recovering from an illness, probably typhoid, he wrote to W. F. Shrapnell 'to dissipate sadness and fill up my leisure hours, I have been collecting my scattered thoughts on the subject of the migration of birds, having long promised a paper to the Royal Society. Can you furnish me with any facts respecting this matter that I do not possess?' The record in the published paper of pigeons flying daily from Holland to the coast of Norfolk was given to Jenner in a letter written by Nathaniel Thornbury on 22 March 1795. Writing to J. F. Blumenbach in September 1801 he mentioned that his observations on the migration of birds had not yet been published: 'I shall, if possible, present a paper on the subject to the Royal Society this winter'. These years

1794–1801 seem to cover the period of his active interest in this question.

The first draft of the Cuckoo essay, February 1787, belonging to the Royal Society, contains at its end a short essay 'On the emigration of birds' in which Jenner suggested that the sole purpose of migration is for birds to propagate their young, noted that they often leave while food is still plentiful, and showed why the hypothesis that they hibernate is untenable; this essay was omitted from the published 'Cuckoo' paper of 1788, where he promised a separate paper on migration, as though it were nearly ready. His preoccupation with cowpox no doubt prevented him from finishing the paper to his own satisfaction, but its arguments are complete as they stand and do not appear to have needed much editing by George Jenner, who wrote in his introductory note 'It had long been the intention of my Uncle to lay the accompanying observations before the Royal Society'. This note was dated within a fortnight of Jenner's death, and addressed to Sir Humphry Davy PRS, a personal friend of Edward Jenner.

The intention of the paper was not to give a general history of migration, but to bring forward some facts hitherto unnoticed, with respect to the *cause* which excites the bird. Jenner expounded the reality of migration, arguing against the hypothesis that birds go into a state of torpor in this country when they disappear. He gave evidence for their ability to make very long flights, and described his experiments in marking the claws of swifts, which had been done on Hunter's advice to check the return of birds to the same place year after year. He provided clear evidence that birds cannot live under water (for it was then believed even by naturalists that some special physiological adaptation enabled birds to hibernate at the bottom of ponds), showing how diving-birds are easily drowned in nets or under ice, and Newfoundland dogs never stay more than thirty seconds under water. Jenner concluded that recurrent change of habitat by birds follows cyclical enlargement of their sexual organs, and they migrate for scarcely any other purpose than to produce an offspring. Dissection shows that the progressive arrival of migrating birds is due to the testes and ovaria being in very different states of progressive forwardness: their return 'home' follows the shrinkage of their sexual organs. He noticed their need for warmth.

Lawrence Kilham's paper (1973), already quoted in connection with Jenner's study of the cuckoo, particularly praised the originality of Jenner's opinions. He saw that Jenner's close observation of bird behaviour in spring made him conclude that 'some new agency was working upon the constitution' and rightly identify this as a seasonal change in the sexual organs of both sexes. 'The true cause of migration' was thus an instinctive need for a better breeding environment; since food is more abundant in spring when birds migrate, Jenner discarded the general belief that want of food causes migration.

John Hunter's Museum contains three preparations made by Jenner to demonstrate the alterations in size of the testes of cuckoos, with one showing the testes of a rook, and two dissections by him of cuckoos' ovaria; these were purchased by the Royal College of Surgeons after the Museum came into its care.

The second part of the paper deals with winter birds of passage and the partially migratory. Temporary winter migrations may be due to sparsity of food – redwings and fieldfares, for instance, feed on worms and insects unobtainable from the ground in hard frost, and eat haws very sparingly, 'contrary to the statements of every naturalist I have ever had access to'. This part ends with a rhetorical discourse on birdsong and its appropriate times, including Jenner's observation that first the robin, not the lark, sings in the early morning.

The third part recorded that John Hunter first demonstrated the different sizes of the testes of birds at different seasons, and Jenner added his own further observations. He noted the comparative smallness of the testes in birds which remain but a short time paired with the female, compared with those that live in the connubial state much longer. Jenner corrected Erasmus Darwin's statement that cuckoos feed their nestlings; the birds which his friend saw were goat-suckers [nightjars].

The paper was printed in the *Philosophical Transactions* early in 1824, and reset as a separate pamphlet the same year; L. C. Froriep's journal of natural history and medicine *Notizen* included an abstract in German in its March issue; George Jenner's son had the paper reprinted in Gloucestershire in 1882.

138[113]  Some Observations on the Migration of Birds. By the late Edward Jenner, M.D. F.R.S., with an Introductory Letter to Sir Humphry Davy, Bart. Pres.R.S. By the Rev. G. C. Jenner. Read November 27 1823, *Philosophical Transactions of the Royal Society of London. For the year MDCCCXXIV. Part 1.* London: Printed by W. Nicol . . . and sold by G. and W. Nicol . . . Printers to the Royal Society. MDCCCXXIV. [Vol. 114, article 2].

RUNNING TITLE: The late Dr. Jenner on the migration of birds.

COLLATION: 4°: C2ᵃ–G2ᵇ; pp. 11–44.

CONTENTS: p. 12 Title-heading, G. C. Jenner's note dated May 29, 1823, text begins [I] at line 11; p. 30, line 18: II. Winter Birds of Passage; p. 40, line 1: III. Mr. John Hunter, my late valued friend . . . ; p. 42, line 23: To recapitulate . . .

COPIES USED: Royal Society and RCS.

**139[114]**     Some Observations on the Migration of Birds [*rule*] By the late Edward Jenner, M.D. F.R.S. With an introductory letter to Sir Humphry Davy, Bart. by the Rev. G. C. Jenner. [*rule*] From the *Philosophical Transactions*. London: [*double rule*] Printed by William Nicol, Cleveland Row, St James's. 1824.

COLLATION: 4°:A–B⁴, D–E⁴, F²; 36 pp. 300 mm. Plain blue wrappers.

CONTENTS: A1ᵃ Title; A1ᵇ Order by W. T. Brande, Sec. R.S., as to reprinting; A2ᵃ–2ᵇ, p. [3]–4 Heading and introductory note; A2ᵇ–D3ᵇ, pp. 4–22 text part I; D3ᵇ–E4ᵃ, p. 22, line 18 – p. 31 text part II; E4ᵇ–F2ᵇ, pp. 32–36 text part III; F2ᵇ, p. 36 colophon below rule: Printed by W. Nicol, Cleveland Row, St James's.

COPIES:Bristol PL, Cheltenham PL, RCPE, WHM (2), NLM, MiU (Crummer), ViU, YMH.

COPIES USED: WHM, both copies.

NOTE: ViU copy inscribed: "The Rev. Doctor Davies from his affectionate cousin G. C. Jenner."

**140[115]**     Some Observations on the Migration of Birds by Edward Jenner, M.D. F.R.S., the Rev. George Charles Jenner, MD, of the Medical Society of Paris, and Geo. C. Jenner.

COLLATION: 8°:front wrapper, 16 pp. 18 cm. Without signatures or watermark.

CONTENTS: Title on wrapper: p. 1 Heading as title, text begins; p. 10 Winter birds of passage; p. 16 text ends, signed Geo. C. Jenner, 'Address to a Robin', Edward Jenner, M.D. F.R.S. [20 lines]. [A proof or trial issue, 1882?].

COPY: Gloucester PL (Roland Austin, *Catalogue of the Gloucestershire Collection*, no. 14,752) – information (1948) from P. W. Bennett, City Librarian.

SOME OBSERVATIONS

ON

# THE MIGRATION OF BIRDS.

_____

BY

### THE LATE EDWARD JENNER,

**M. D. F. R. S.**

WITH AN

### INTRODUCTORY LETTER TO SIR HUMPHRY DAVY, BART.

BY

### THE REV. G. C. JENNER.

_____

FROM THE

PHILOSOPHICAL TRANSACTIONS.

## LONDON :

PRINTED BY WILLIAM NICOL, CLEVELAND-ROW, ST. JAMES'S.

1824.

Migration of Birds (First edition 1824)

141[116]     [*In double rule border*]: Some Observations . . . [as 140] 1882.
[*rule*] J. Iles, printer, Chipping Sodbury.

COLLATION: 8°:16 pp. 18 cm. Blue wrappers.

COPY USED: YMH (Cushing collection).


142[117]     Über die Wanderungen der Vögel . . . Dr. Edward Jenner
. . . eine Abhandlung . . . von dessen Neffen H. C. Jenner . . . ein kurzer
Auszug, *Notizen aus dem Gebiete der Natur- und Heilkunde*, von Ludwig
Friedrich v. Froriep . . . Erfurt, 6 (Marz 1824), nr. 19, columns 289–93.

COPY USED: RCS.


## II   LETTERS TO S. B. LABATT

A small group of Jenner's letters was published in 1859 when Hamilton
Labatt, a Dublin surgeon, printed in a journal article and later as a
pamphlet five letters from Jenner to his father, Dr Samuel Bell Labatt, who
had been Director of the Dublin Cow-pock Institution. The letters are
dated: 11 February 1807, 8 February 1810 from Catherine Jenner on behalf
of her husband, 20 January 1811, 8 July 1811, 19 February 1814, 6 January
1821; all deal with vaccination. Hamilton Labatt stated that his father did
not preserve the whole correspondence, so that he could only publish such
of Jenner's letters as had appeared among his father's papers, and that the
greater part of the third letter had been printed by S. B. Labatt in *An address
to the medical practitioners of Ireland on the subject of vaccination*, second
edition, Dublin 1840, pp. 46–48.

In his letter of 6 January 1821 Jenner wrote 'I am about shortly to publish
a circular and I shall send you one as soon as I can get it printed'. A letter
from Jenner to Labatt of 19 February 1809 was printed in the *Report of the
Cow-pock Institution, Dublin* for 1809. Arnold C. Klebs's copy of Jenner's
*Facts* (1808) at YMH is inscribed by Jenner to S. B. Labatt, for whom see
A. A. McCabe, 'Samuel Bell Labatt', *Irish Journal of Medical Science*, 435
(1965) 97–105.

**143[118]**     Letters addressed by Edward Jenner, M.D., to the late Samuel Bell Labatt, M.D., of Dublin, on the subject of vaccination, edited by Hamilton Labatt, *Dublin Quarterly Journal of Medical Science*, 27 (no. 54) (1 May 1859), 467–72.

**144[119]**     Letters addressed by Edward Jenner, M.D., to the late Samuel Bell Labatt, M.D., of Dublin, on the subject of Vaccination. Edited by Hamilton Labatt, A.B., F.R.C.S.I. Dublin: printed at the University Press, by M. H. Gill, 1859.

COLLATION: 8°:[A]¹–B⁴; 10 pp. 213 mm.

CONTENTS: A1ᵃ Title: A1ᵇ (From the Dublin Quarterly Journal of Medical Science, May 1859); B1ᵃ–4ᵇ, pp. 3–10 Introduction and Letters.

RUNNING TITLE: Letters from Edward Jenner, M.D., to the late Dr. Labatt.

COPY USED: RSM.

III   THE CRUMMER NOTEBOOK

The University of Michigan Library at Ann Arbor possesses a manuscript in the hand of Jenner's nephew William Davies, bequeathed by LeRoy Crummer MD of Omaha, Nebraska, well-known as a collector of books. It is a transcript of 'Fragments, Quotations, etc. etc., found in pocket books and on detached scraps of paper belonging to Dr. Jenner. These were chiefly written in pencil by the Doctor when he travelled alone in his carriage'. Some passages seem to have been transcribed from the Hellman Notebook.

   The dated entries range from 1788 to 1823, but there are few before 1809. The notes are of great variety: philosophic meditations, quotations, prescriptions, weather records, diary entries, etc. There are many notes on vaccination, and other medical observations. At the end is a copy of answers to an insurance questionnaire. Crummer commented that his notebook gives a view of the range of Jenner's interests, many of which extended far beyond the medical horizon. He printed this MS in 1929 having 'sometime since' acquired it among a portion of the material used by Baron in preparing his *Life of Jenner*.

**145[120]**    Copy of Jenner Notebook, edited by LeRoy Crummer, M.D., Omaha, Nebraska, *Annals of Medical History*, new series, 1 (July 1929), 403–48.


## IV    THE ROYAL COLLEGE OF PHYSICIANS NOTEBOOK

The Royal College of Physicians of London possesses a notebook in Jenner's hand containing notes on natural history and comparative medicine, which include his journal from 26 April to 22 July 1787, the period of his discoveries concerning the cuckoo. The contents are: Journal 26 April – 22 July 1787 [observations on birds, especially cuckoos]; Experiments continued, 9 November 1793; Hydatids, 10 February – 9 May 1796; Dogs – distemper, May 1796 – 29 April 1806; another hydatid case is inserted between the first and second distemper cases.

The observations on the cuckoo were used for Jenner's Royal Society paper of 1788, but the Notebook does not record all the detail given in the finished paper. His experiments in the prevention of distemper have been discussed already. His work on hydatids, here recorded from 1796, occupied his thoughts for a great part of his life. They are watery cysts caused by invertebrate infestation, usually containing tapeworm larvae, and were first recorded in 1683 as cysts containing 'insects'. Jenner wrote here 'I long ago conceived that the true tuberculous consumption originated by hydatids getting into the lungs and there forming tubercles'. This was a false assumption, but bacteria were quite unknown and the tubercle bacillus discovered only in 1882. He also reported hydatids occurring in the interstices of the muscular fibres in a hog: 'I pointed out this fact to Mr. Hunter in the year 1786'. This may refer to Hunter's paper 'Some observations on digestion' in his *Observations on the Animal Oeconomy* (1786) where he mentioned 'a piece of the intestine of a hog which has a number of air-bladders in it', with a drawing of it on an engraved plate facing p. 189; the 'explanation' of the plate states that 'It was sent to me by my friend Mr. Jenner, surgeon at Berkeley, who informed me that this appearance is found very frequently upon the intestines of hogs killed in the summer months'. On 28 July 1790 Jenner reported a case of hydatids successfully treated with oil of turpentine to the Gloucestershire Medical Society, but Hunter wrote to him on the following 8 December 'I have just now forgot the case of the hydatids; but if there was anything that struck me, I dare say it was laid by. They are frequently in the kidneys, but I should doubt your oil of turpentine having any merit in bringing them away. My reason for supposing them animals is because they move after they have been extracted. I have taken them out of the head or brain of a sheep and they have contracted in different parts of them when put into warm water'.

In the year of this Notebook entry, 1796, Jenner wrote several times to Thomas Beddoes assuring him of his conviction that hydatids formed tubercles in cows' lungs. Beddoes quoted these letters in his *Considerations on the medicinal Use and on the Production of Factitious Airs*, Part 1 [pp. 1–180] by Thomas Beddoes, M.D., Part 2 [pp. 181–220] by James Watt, Engineer. [pp. 221–22 Advertisement; pp. 1–8 Addenda]. Edition the third. Bristol, Bulgin and Rosser, for J. Johnson, London 1796.

A footnote at pp. 177–78 gives *Extracts of letters from Dr. Jenner;* two letters are quoted, the second dated 'Berkeley, January 29, 1796'. Two further letters are quoted in the Addenda, pp. 1–4, the first of them dated 'Kingscote-House, February 9'.

Baron printed a letter of 13 December 1809 in which Jenner wrote to Richard Worthington 'I trust some advantage may one day or another be derived from my having demonstrably made out that what *is* tubercle in the lungs *has been* hydatid'. Jenner was aware of the parasitic origin of hydatid cysts, but seems to have convinced himself of the truth of his hypothesis that tubercles were the same cysts at a later stage. Baron in his *An Enquiry illustrating the Nature of tuberculated Accretions of serous membranes*, 1819, says (p. 123) that Jenner's 'unceasing attention to vaccination interfered with his purpose of writing on hydatids'. There are several references to Jenner in this book (see **151**) although in his *Delineations of the Origin and Progress of various Changes of Structure which occur in Man*, 1828, Baron says that Jenner furnished him only with a general statement of the result of his observations. Jenner was reading Baron's second book on the subject – *Illustrations of the Enquiry respecting Tuberculous Diseases*, 1822 – when he died.

The text of the Notebook was published in 1931 with a descriptive preface by the Harveian Librarian of the College, Dr Arnold Chaplin, and an introduction on 'Edward Jenner as a naturalist' by Dr F. Dawtrey Drewitt, which he used again in his *Life of Edward Jenner* in the same year.

## MANUSCRIPT

Notebook, small 4°, 21 cm, 80 leaves, written in Edward Jenner's hand; bound in boards with leather spine; bookplate and ownership inscription of George Charles Jenner. Given to the College by J. A. Marston MD in 1888.

## PRINTED EDITION

**146[121]**    The Notebook of Edward Jenner in the possession of the Royal College of Physicians of London with an Introduction on Jenner's Work as a Naturalist by F. Dawtrey Drewitt, M.D. (Oxon.), F.R.C.P. formerly on the Committee of the British Ornithologists' Union and on the Council of the Zoological Society of London. Oxford University Press London: Humphrey Milford 1931.

COLLATION: 4°:frontispiece, A–F⁴, G⁶; vii, 49 pp. 21 cm. Grey boards, blue cloth spine: lettered up spine 'The Notebook of Edward Jenner' and at foot 'Oxford'.

CONTENTS: A1ᵃ Half-title: The Notebook of Edward Jenner; Frontispiece facing title: Edward Jenner, M.D. F.R.S. From the portrait by Sir Thomas Lawrence, P.R.A., in the possession of The Royal College of Physicians of London. Emery Walker Ltd. ph. sc.; A2ᵃ Title; A2ᵇ Oxford University Press . . . printed in Great Britain; A3ᵃ–4ᵃ, pp. v–vii Preface [signed] 'A.C.'; B1ᵃ—D1ᵃ pp. 1–17 Edward Jenner, M.D., as a Naturalist [signed] 'F.D.D.'; D2ᵃ—G5ᵃ, pp. 19–49 The Notebook of Edward Jenner; G5ᵇ Printed in Great Britain at the University Press, Oxford by John Johnson, Printer to the University.

## V    THE HELLMAN NOTEBOOK

Dr Alfred M. Hellman of New York acquired during the 1920s a 'home-made copy-book' (17 × 10 cm) on ninety-six leaves in a leather cover, containing 188 pages of miscellaneous memoranda in Jenner's hand; one leaf was missing. The book was ostensibly a diary for 1810–12, but appears to have been used as a general notebook. Dr Hellman afterwards sold the book through Schuman of New York (Catalogue 1, Spring 1937, no. 140).

Miss C. Doris Hellman, well-known as an historian of science, published a transcript of this book while it belonged to her father, with reproductions of several pages and of a drawing by Jenner. Miss Hellman (Mrs Morton Pepper) kindly gave me further particulars.

Several passages were apparently transcribed by William Davies from this notebook into his fair copy of Jenner's notes (**145**) as 'those passages which appear in both notebooks are mostly checked in ink in our notebook'.

The contents include prescriptions, stray thoughts, notes of professional visits, records of vaccinations, and pencil drawings. There is a note on 'staggers' in horses, epigrams and *vers d'occasion* by Jenner, notes on hydatids and on diabetes 'this strange disease'; Jenner asks himself 'Where is the origin of the disease? in the Brain? the Stomach? the Chyme? the Lactials? the Kidneys? most probably in the Brain, the Brain rules the excretions'.

The Notebook is now in the Josiah Trent collection, Medical Center Library, Duke University, Durham, North Carolina.

**147[122]**   An Unpublished Diary of Edward Jenner (1810–1812). Edited by C. Doris Hellman, B.A., New York, *Annals of Medical History*, new series, 3 (July 1931), 412–38.

## VI   THE WELLCOME NOTEBOOKS

The Wellcome Institute for the History of Medicine owns three notebooks among the Jenner papers acquired by Sir Henry Wellcome in 1918 and later:

**148**   Diary of visits to patients, Prescriptions, etc. 1794. In Jenner's hand. MS 3018.

**149**   List of letters, documents, etc. relating to Vaccination received by Dr. Jenner 1801, 1803. In the hand of G. C. Jenner. MS 3020.

**150**   Names of Patients, Dates of visits, Prescriptions 1803. A small notebook in Jenner's hand. MS 3021.

All are described fully in the published *Catalogue* of the Wellcome Manuscripts.

# CHAPTER 6
## Letters

Personages of whom we read only in books seem alive in letters regarding them, whose voices I almost fancy to hear as I read the yellow pages written scores of years since.

W. M. Thackeray, *The Virginians*, 1858.

Edward Jenner described himself as vaccination clerk to the world, but some eight hundred letters surviving from his correspondence are a small harvest compared with those of earlier scientists such as Henry Oldenburg or Marin Mersenne or the thousands of letters written by Voltaire or Horace Walpole. Letters were, however, his chief means of spreading knowledge of vaccination among potential supporters and beyond the medical profession for whom he wrote his books. The letters he received are the fullest record of his worldwide contacts, while his own letters display his wide scientific interests, his sense of mission, his normal optimism and occasional irritation or melancholy. Though he wrote clearly and succinctly when necessary, 'I am too apt', he admitted 'to run into metaphor in my correspondence'.

Much of this correspondence is known only from printed transcripts, particularly the three hundred letters quoted at length in John Baron's biography, yet his autograph letters are not uncommon; they have been preserved and collected since he became famous in middle life. J. M. P. Munaret wrote in his *Iconautographie de Jenner* (1860) 'les autographes de Jenner pèsent de l'or'. The Wellcome Institute's Jenner archive, with some two hundred letters, includes his own drafts or retained copies; they have not been published, but when Sir Henry Wellcome's files of medical letters were first opened about 1947 I was generously allowed to make a provisional list for my *Bio-Bibliography*. From Henry Barton Jacobs's Jenner collection of more than one hundred letters, which he gave to the Welch Library in the Institute of the History of Medicine at Baltimore, partial texts of thirty-eight letters were printed, some by Dr Jacobs in 1919 and more by Dr Genevieve Miller in 1948. Dr Miller's edition of the whole series was published in 1983; she generously gave me in advance a calendar of the correspondence with a draft of her introduction, where she shows that the letters, running from 1785 to 1823, give an intimate glimpse of Jenner's professional and private life. The book is the most lifelike picture of Jenner's character and interests, drawn by his own pen.

Through his first twenty years of practice, before vaccination became wholly absorbing, Jenner's main exchange of letters was with his close friend and former master John Hunter. Each kept the other man's letters, but Jenner's to Hunter were destroyed, before Baron could use them for his biography, probably in Everard Home's bonfire of Hunter's papers in 1823. Fifty-one letters from Hunter to Jenner are known; many were printed by John Baron in his *Life of Edward Jenner* (1827–38) and by Drewry Ottley in his 'Life of John Hunter' in Hunter's *Works* (1835); thirty-one have been edited with some facsimiles by E. H. Cornelius and A. J. Harding Rains as *Letters from the Past* (Royal College of Surgeons, 1976).

Another extended series, Jenner's letters to Alexander Marcet, who practised in London, is divided between the Royal Society of Medicine in London and the Jacobs collection in Baltimore; Marcet was an Edinburgh-trained Swiss physician with many Continental friends. The Royal College of Surgeons owns thirty-six autographs from the archive which Baron gathered for his *Life of Jenner*; copies and autograph scraps, also from Baron's collection, were owned by LeRoy Crummer of Omaha, who described them in *Annals of Medical History* (1929) but did not leave them in his bequest of Jennerian books to the University of Michigan. The Wellcome collection includes much of Jenner's correspondence with his west-country friend Thomas Pruen and his Dutch translator L. Davids, with James Moore of the National Vaccine Institution and Charles Murray of the Royal Jennerian Society; the College of Physicians of Philadelphia owns more of his letters to Murray, partly published by their donor S. Weir Mitchell in the College's *Transactions* (1900). The correspondence with his critic Jan Ingenhousz was printed in the Dutch periodical *Janus* (1964) by P. W. van der Pas.

Jenner's letters to the press and to a few personal correspondents, such as S. B. Labatt of the Dublin Cow-Pock Institute, printed in his lifetime or soon after, have been described already among his publications about vaccination; personal letters were also printed in biographies of his contemporaries from as early as T. J. Pettigrew's *Memoirs of J. C. Lettsom* (1817), while further letters have been published piecemeal in recent times. He sent advice when consulted by clergymen or lay people, for he encouraged the parson or the lady of the manor to vaccinate in country places. He corresponded with scientists, from the President of the Royal Society to amateur naturalists in his neighbourhood; he kept in touch with leading London surgeons: John Abernethy, Gilbert Blane, Henry Cline and Everard Home; with prominent physicians: William Heberden in London, James Currie at Liverpool, Caleb Parry and his son Charles at Bath; with many physicians abroad, particularly Jean de Carro at Vienna, and in North America with his old friend John Clinch, who had settled in Newfoundland, and with Benjamin Waterhouse, founding professor of the Harvard Faculty of Medicine; but only a few letters survive from each of these exchanges. To many of these correspondents he enclosed threads dipped in cowpox exudate, substituting from about 1804 small ivory lancets. Mr Eric Quayle kindly sent me in 1983 a photocopy of an undated letter in his collection from Jenner to Mr Tuke [perhaps William Tuke, founder of The Retreat at York], to which such an impregnated thread is still attached. In his campaign for universal vaccination Jenner wrote to the Empress who promoted it in Russia, to the King of Spain who sent a vaccinating mission round his South American dominions, and at least twice to Napoleon using the influence of his reputation to seek release of Englishmen interned in France during the war.

His simple generosity brought him into direct contact with the Indian Chiefs of the Five Nations in Canada. Benjamin Waterhouse, who vaccinated with success round Boston from 1799, had sent instructions to the President of the United States, Thomas Jefferson, for vaccinating the Indians near Washington in 1801. The Indian Department at Montreal similarly provided vaccination for a group of the Abenaquis at St Francis in Upper Canada in 1803, and in 1807 Jenner sent a copy of the Royal Jennerian Society's *Address for 1803*, which he inscribed 'For the Chiefs of the Five Nations from Dr. Jenner', to Francis Gore, the Lieutenant-Governor of Upper Canada, who organized a large-scale vaccination of Indians on the River Credit and at the Head of the Lake; the book is preserved in the Public Archives at Ottawa and was described by J. J. Heagerty in *Four Centuries of Medical History in Canada* (1928). The Chiefs wrote to thank Jenner for his help and sent him a large piece of wampum (though it was not generally known in England that these woven bead patterns embodied coded messages); the Chiefs' letter with their pictograph signatures was published in the *Edinburgh Medical and Surgical Journal* for April 1812 and again by Baron (1838).

The first edition of this *Bio-Bibliography* included a chronological list of nearly seven hundred letters from or to Jenner, with detail of publication or location of autographs; in the three decades since then another hundred have come to my notice in book-dealers' catalogues or by information from collectors and librarians; many more autographs no doubt remain unrecorded, with transcripts overlooked in printed books. Such information can be better recorded now in a computer; perhaps some large library or historical institute will assume the task. Publication of the longer correspondences would prove interesting and informative, but there is a monotony of reiterated advice on vaccinating in many of the separate letters.

## CHAPTER 7

# Miscellaneous Writings

The smallpox – that venomous scourge which, thanks to Jenner, every village Esculapius can tame.

Sir Walter Scott, *The Heart of Midlothian*, 1818.

## I PROSE WRITINGS

Jenner's family placed his unpublished manuscripts in John Baron's hands when they chose him as biographer. He and Jenner had been friends for nearly fifteen years and had met sometimes in professional consultation, as he told in *An Enquiry illustrating the Nature of Tuberculated Accretions of Serous Membranes* (1819) where also he had quoted a few observations sent to him by Jenner:

**151[123]**     Report on the case of W. F. Shrapnell; observations on tubercles in the liver and among the other viscera of the pig; on cases of scirrhous tumour (pp. 47–49, 51–52, 131–32, 158–64).

Baron published other extracts from Jenner's journals and notebooks in his *Life of Edward Jenner*; they cover a wide range of Jenner's interests. Among them are the memorials on behalf of Englishmen interned abroad during the Napoleonic war, and a short essay on the geology of the Berkeley district. Jenner collected fossils from boyhood; in the 1780s he sent specimens to John Hunter and exchanged others with Caleb Parry. He joined John Baron and other friends in geologizing expeditions about 1812–14; this 'Barrow Hill Club' met at the Bell Inn, Frampton a few miles north of Berkeley. Even as late as 1818 he corresponded with John Walcott who had published *Descriptions of Petrifactions found near Bath* nearly forty years earlier (1779) and in 1821 he sent Charles Parry specimens he had collected near Berkeley. Dr Hugh Torrens of Keele University has given me (1983) several references to the geological literature from 1820 to 1840 where Jenner's geological knowledge and fossil collection are mentioned. Soon after he died, his family gave the Bristol Institution in 1823 his *Plesiosaurus* specimen, one of the first recorded.

### WRITINGS PRINTED IN BARON'S *LIFE OF JENNER*

**152[124]** A snowstorm on 3 January 1786 (1, 72–73). Jenner describes his ride through a blizzard, his collapse and recovery.

**153[125]** Proposals by Dr Jenner for a public Institution for Vaccine Inoculation. London, 16 March 1800 (1, 367–69). Sent to Lord Egremont, this led to the founding of the National Vaccine Institution.

**154[126]** On the geology of the Berkeley district (2, 443).

**155[127]** Observations on the night-blowing primrose, 7 April 1818. (2, 444–45); discusses the economy of nature in providing food for night-flying moths.

**156[128]** Miscellaneous notes on medicine (2, 445–46) and religion (2, 446–47).

**157[129]** Extracts from journals: Jenner's visit to London to publish the Inquiry, 1798 (1, 149); on cow-pox, 1799 (1, 122 note); on vaccination, 1801 (1, 449); on his country occupations, 1803 (1, 575); on the vaccination of Lord Grosvenor's child, 1817 (2, 267).

**158[130]** Miscellaneous notes on animal poxes (1, 237–38 note), on horsepox (1, 242), and on variolation and vaccination (1, 246).

**159[131]** Thanks returned to the Committee of the House of Commons, 1802 (1, 521).

**160[132]** Memorial to the King of Spain on behalf of Mr Powell a prisoner of war; memorials to the Emperor of Austria on behalf of Mr Sinclair, interned; and to Napoleon on behalf of Mr Gold and Mr Garland, interned (2, 114–15).

**161[133]** A testimonial for an English traveller in France during the war, 1 July 1810 (2, 116).

**162[134]** Statement to Baron on the species of mental torture endured before appearance at a public meeting, 1811 (2, 162).

**163[135]** The expenses arising from his discovery till 1811 (2, 163).

**164[136]** Audience of the Emperor of Russia in London, 1814 (2, 206–07).

**165[137]** Inscription in a Bible given to his god-daughter Augusta Bertie Parry (2, 295).

**166[138]** A Prayer – one of some fragments of prayers, written under affliction (2, 295–6).

**167[139]** Last writing on vaccination, on the back of a letter with postmark 14 January 1823 (2, 311): 'My opinion of vaccination is precisely as it was when I promulgated the discovery. It is not in the least strengthened by any event that has happened, for it could gain no strength; it is not in the least weakened, for if the failures you speak of had not happened, the truth of my assertions respecting those coincidences which occasioned them would not have been made out'. This had been copied by

Baron for Louis Valentin, who quoted it in French in his *Notice historique sur le Docteur Jenner*, second edition, 1824.

**168[140]**    Last note, 24 January 1823: the case of his friend Joyner Ellis dying after exposure to severe cold. (Baron 2, 312).

**169[141]**    Letter to one of the chief anti-vaccinists (ca. 1806), not published, and only mentioned by Baron (2, 64). Ludwig Pfeiffer's *Jenner Literatur Katalog*, (Weimar 1891) and the *Catalogue* of Frederick Mockler's Jenner collection (Bristol 1893) both mention a pamphlet of this title and date, probably James Moore's answer to William Rowley, printed by G. Woodfall for John Murray (1806) which Baron may have attributed to Jenner.

Writings by Jenner, not all autograph, and many papers concerning his family are recorded in detail by S. A. J. Moorat in his *Catalogue of Western Manuscripts in the Wellcome Historical Medical Library, II: written after 1650 A.D.* (1973); they include: An Essay on Marriage, holograph 1783 (MS 3014); Drafts for legal documents, with holograph notes by Jenner – Statement of a case for libel, 1808 (MS 3024); Two drafts of An Act for preventing the Spread of the Smallpox 1808 (MS 3025); Heads of the Will of Dr Jenner, ca. 1810 (MS 3026); An Inventory and Valuation of the Household Property of Dr Jenner at Berkeley and Cheltenham, February 1823 (MS 3027).

The British Library's copy of Baron's *Illustrations of the Enquiry respecting Tuberculous Diseases* (1822) has between title-page and dedication a folded leaf with Jenner's autograph notes on all four pages. Jenner characterized the book as highly serviceable and asked a series of questions arising on particular points. The dedication to Jenner is dated 26 November 1822; Baron inscribed the flyleaf: 'This is the dedication copy which I sent to Dr. Jenner. The remarks in his handwriting and the Red Tape were in it, as they are now, when he died. The remarks were intended for me and I got permission to carry them away together with the book on the morning of the death of my venerated and illustrious friend'.

Jenner gave evidence at a murder trial in 1796 and at the Berkeley Peerage Claim in the House of Lords in 1811; his verbal evidence was recorded in the reports of these occasions. He was concerned, as a magistrate, in the preliminaries for the trial of John Allen who had shot a gamekeeper in 1816, but he was not called to give evidence.

Henry Jenner had been called one night in 1794 to attend William Reed, who was dying in a cottage near Berkeley, while travelling from Dorset to Wales with his wife Anne. Henry diagnosed poisoning and confirmed his suspicion by feeding Reed's vomit to a dog which quickly died; this was corroborated by Edward Jenner. At the trial of Anne Reed at Gloucester in 1796, Edward and Henry both gave evidence which is recorded in a report in Gloucester Public Library.

After Lord Berkeley's death in 1810 his eldest son claimed his right to the peerage on the strength of what proved to be a forged registration of his parents' marriage in 1785; they were not married till 1796, and the peerage was awarded to the son born in 1797. Edward Jenner gave evidence before the Committee of Privileges at the first hearing on 7 March and again at the last on 18 June 1811. His answers are recorded in *A Narrative of the Minutes of Evidence respecting the Claim to the Berkeley Peerage* (1811). Both episodes are described in some detail, with discussion of Jenner's role in them, by Saunders (1982).

## II  VERSE WRITINGS

Edward Jenner enjoyed writing light verse: epigrams on local people and events or songs for his convivial clubs, with a few more serious poems on themes from nature. *The Gentleman's Magazine*, complaining in 1819 (vol. 89, p. 239) of the vanity of amateur poets in publishing their verses, suggested that they ought to circulate them privately: 'we know a celebrated man, Dr. Jenner, who occasionally writes poems, but prints them upon half-sheets as gifts among his friends'; the Wellcome Institute Library has two such separately printed poems. For the first edition of this *Bio-Bibliography* (1951) I compiled a list of sixty-eight sets of verses by Jenner: eighteen autographs from the Hellman Notebook, nineteen contemporary transcripts among John Baron's papers at the Royal College of Surgeons, fourteen others printed in Baron's *Life of Edward Jenner*, and twenty from a printed pamphlet in the Alderman Library of the University of Virginia, with a few from other books. Since then a second printed pamphlet has come to notice containing nine poems, all but one repeating items in the first pamphlet, while the *Catalogue* of the Wellcome Manuscripts, published in 1973, records two notebooks containing transcripts of ninety-four poems. Jenner's three best sets of verses have been reprinted from time to time: *Signs of Rain*, a summary of country lore, and the two *Addresses to a Robin*, one praising 'the sweetest of the feather'd throng' and the other abusing the 'sturdy ruffian'. Thomas Fosbroke printed a Latin version of the last in his *Berkeley Manuscripts* (1821), and John Latham's version of *Signs of Rain* appeared separately, after his printed Latin poems (1853).

## MANUSCRIPT VERSES

'A Legendary Tale', in the hand of William Davies, the younger, about 1790. Wellcome MS 3015.

'Poems mostly by Edward Jenner', a collection in the signed hand of William Davies: two notebooks containing 94 poems, of which 68 are initialled 'E.J.' including 38 not in the 1951 list. Wellcome MSS 3016–17.

Autograph verses in the *Hellman Notebook*, pp. 158–75.

Contemporary transcripts of 19 poems: John Baron's papers, Royal College of Surgeons of England.

'To William Hobday R.A.', autograph at Royal Society of Medicine [about 1821].

## PRINTED VERSES

**170[142]**     [Poems].
Pamphlet, 30 leaves (originally 32?), wanting title page and date; 20 poems by Edward Jenner. University of Virginia, Charlottesville, Alderman Library.

**171[143]**     Poems never before published, Worcester 1804.
Pamphlet of poems by members of the Sheridan family, with 9 by Edward Jenner. Described in the *Daily Telegraph*, London, 12 and 13 September 1951 and sold at Sotheby's 15 July 1952, lot 278.

172–73[144–45]    Edward Jenner and his servant; My Spanish Segar.
Undated leaflets at Wellcome Institute Library.


174    John Baron *Life of Edward Jenner* (1827–38): verses at 1, 20–25, and
2, 434–42.


## III   RELICS AND SPECIAL COLLECTIONS

Jenner bequeathed his vaccination papers and the diplomas and other gifts,
with which he had been honoured in profusion, as heirlooms to his family.
A large part of these passed into the collection of a family connection,
Frederick Mockler, and were bought by Sir Henry Wellcome in 1919. The
Wellcome Institute thus possesses the largest collection of Jenner's books,
letters and papers, with anatomical specimens, portraits, medicine-
cabinets and other personal relics. They were described in the printed
Catalogues of the *Exhibition commemorating the centenary of the death of Dr.
Edward Jenner*, February 1923, and the *Exhibition commemorating the
bicentenary of Edward Jenner*, May 1949.

   The Royal College of Surgeons of England owns, besides the manuscripts already described, part of John Baron's collection of Jenner's papers
with leaflets and pamphlets about vaccination which had been sent to
Jenner. Dr Sydney Turner of Gloucester gave the College a small silver
box inscribed 'Edwd. Jenner Surgeon Berkeley', which is believed to have
held the squares of glass on which he preserved vaccine. Jenner's preparations in the Hunterian Museum at the College have been mentioned
already in connection with his natural history writings.

   The important Jenner manuscripts at the Royal College of Physicians of
London, his natural history notebook and the papers of the Gloucestershire Medical Society, have been described in previous chapters; the
College has also a medicine-chest of Jenner's, and a horn of the cow from
which Jenner is said to have taken his first cowpox virus. The cow's hide
was given by his son Colonel Robert Jenner to St George's Hospital
Medical School; the hide of another cow, which also provided cowpox
virus, was for many years in the chemist's shop of Anderson and Virgo at
Worcester.

   The Society of Apothecaries of London possesses the gold casket in
which the diploma of the Freedom of the City of London was presented

to Jenner. He was awarded many such honorary citizenships; George Jenner's list of them, now at the Royal College of Surgeons of England, was printed by Baron.

Dr Henry Barton Jacobs, eminent physician at Baltimore, gave his library to the Welch Institute of the History of Medicine at Johns Hopkins University on its foundation in 1939. Dr and Mrs Jacobs were friends of Sir William Osler and are mentioned many times in his notes in the *Bibliotheca Osleriana* Catalogue. The Jacobs collection is rich in the literature of preventive medicine, and includes an extensive series of editions of Jenner's writings and a gathering of his autograph letters second only to Sir Henry Wellcome's; these letters have now been worthily edited by Dr Genevieve Miller (1983).

Jenner inscribed many copies of his various publications as gifts, and gave silver and porcelain and replicas of his bust to special friends and supporters. A silver box inlaid with gold and inscribed 'Edwd Jenner to Bn Waterhouse' is in the Countway Library of Medicine, Boston (Harvard Medical School collection); the porcelain which he sent to Waterhouse was described in the *Catalogue of the Harvard Tercentenary Exhibition of Furniture* . . . 1936. Another silver box was taken from Jenner to Jean de Carro at Vienna by Joseph Frank, as he recalled in his *Reise nach Paris, London, usw* (1804–05); de Carro later gave it to the National Museum at Prague, where it was brought to notice by Dr Vladislav Kruta during the 1950s. Jenner gave a silver inkstand to the poet Robert Bloomfield, in gratitude for his vaccination poem *Good Tidings, or News from the Farm* (1804); a standish with three silver mounted cut-glass ink-wells, which Jenner used, was given by Samuel Weir Mitchell to the College of Physicians of Philadelphia; it is reproduced with other Jennerian relics in the College's pamphlet *Custodianship of Rush, Jenner, Pasteur, Lister, Curie Mementos* (1920).

There are several important groups of Jenner's publications in the great North American medical libraries; particularly interesting are Sir William Osler's collection in his Library at Montreal, the Harvey Cushing and Arnold C. Klebs collections at Yale Medical Historical Library, the LeRoy Crummer collection at the University of Michigan Library, Ann Arbor, and a volume combining ten rare editions of Jenner's books at the Alderman Library, University of Virginia, Charlottesville.

Besides the copies which Jenner inscribed to friends, noticed in the bibliographical descriptions of each book, a few association copies of interest have been recorded: Sir Charles Morgan, well-known in the early nineteenth century as physician and philosopher, and husband of the Irish novelist Sydney Owenson, bought a copy of the *Inquiry*, second edition, when it came out while he was a medical student at Cambridge; it is now at the Royal College of Physicians of Ireland. A copy of the *Inquiry*, third edition, was looted from a plantation house in Virginia during the British-American war of 1813, and given then to the British naval surgeon Peter Wilson, who took it to New Zealand where he settled in 1841, probably the first copy of Jenner's work in the southern hemisphere; it is still there in private hands (information from A. C. Hayton FRCP of New Plymouth, and Gail Lambert *Peter Wilson, Colonial Surgeon* 1981).

Dr Ludwig Pfeiffer of Weimar formed a large library of vaccination literature and published a catalogue in 1891, with a second pamphlet describing the related medals, portraits and illustrations concerning Jenner, smallpox and vaccine (Tubingen 1896); he then sold his collections in Russia, where they are believed to be in the University Library at Tomsk.

Frederick Mockler's collection of the Jenner heirlooms was exhibited several times before it was bought by Sir Henry Wellcome; catalogues were issued at Bristol 1893, London 1894 and Cardiff 1896. The Gloucester City Library owns much of Jennerian interest, described in the *Catalogue of the Gloucestershire Collection* by Roland Austin (1928). The Library of the London School of Hygiene has a large smallpox and vaccination collection, developed from the library presented by Dr Richard James Reece in 1929.

Exhibitions of books and relics of Jenner have usually been displayed at the celebrations of anniversaries: the centenary of his first vaccination, in London, St Petersburg and Tokyo (1896); of his death, in London and Paris (1923); and the bicentenary of his birth, in London, Gloucester and elsewhere (1949); and at Berkeley and Cheltenham (1982). The Jenner Trust established by physicians in Gloucestershire opened the Jenner Museum at Berkeley in 1967; also at Berkeley a filmed 'biography' of Jenner was produced with local actors by the Golden Unicorn Film Unit of Bristol, through the enthusiasm of Canon Eric Gethyn Jones, then Rector of Berkeley.

## IV  WRITINGS OF GEORGE AND HENRY JENNER

Jenner was helped in his scientific and medical work by his two nephews George Charles and Henry, sons of his elder brother Henry, Rector of Rockhampton. George was a clergyman and MD; Henry, a surgeon and later MD, had been apprenticed to his uncle, was one of John Hunter's last pupils, and ultimately succeeded to the practice at Berkeley.

George Jenner reported some of his own vaccination cases and some from John Clinch, with whom he had worked in Newfoundland; 'On Vaccine', *Medical and Physical Journal*, 5 (1801), 401–02. He published in 1805 the *Evidence at large . . . with the Debate* on his uncle's claim for Parliamentary reward, and edited Edward Jenner's *Some Observations on the Migration of Birds* in 1824.

Henry Jenner wrote several pamphlets, most of them in support of vaccination. His publications included:

[Successful use of 'Yellow Bark' in a case of ague] Extract of a letter from Mr. Jenner at Penswic [Painswick], in John Relph *An Inquiry into a new Species of Peruvian Bark . . . the Yellow Bark*, London 1794, pp. 155–56.

*An Address to the Public on the Advantages of Vaccine Inoculation, with the objections to it refuted*. Bristol, Bath and London [1799], 19 pp. WHM copy has authorial corrections on pp. 4 and 15, and two other issues [1800?], one on grey paper with the p. 4 correction printed, the other on white paper with printed 'price 2s.' added. The same (abstract): *Medical and Physical Journal* 4 (1800), 71, and Ueber die Vorzuge der Kuhpockenimpfung, *Physischmedicinisches Journal* 2 (1808), 63–75.

*Address to the Inhabitants of Bristol on the subject of Vaccine Inoculation*. Bristol 1801.

*[Memoir] of the late Dr. Jenner*, 1823 and 1824, see in Chapter 8, Biographies 14 and 22.

*Advice to Mothers and Nurses on the Management of Children*. 1826.

*An Essay on the salutary Influence of Counter-excitement in preventing and curing Morbid Diseases, with some Observations on Poisons*. Dursley, W. Rickards, 1835, 24 pp. The *Essay* (pp. 5–17) is dated 14 February 1835; the pamphlet includes (pp. 9–24) *Cholera morbus* dated 22 December 1831.

'Revaccinations in 1839 of persons previously vaccinated by me and the revaccinations also by me only'. Berkeley, 8 August 1839. Autograph MS at RCS; published in part in *Observations and Recommendations relative to Vaccination*, Bristol [1839?] 8 pp. The *Observations* (pp. 1–5) are dated 14 February 1836; at pp. 6–8 'Some of the cases relative to vaccination . . . under my own observation in . . . Berkeley only'.

'On the infection of diseases'. Berkeley 1840. Autograph MS at RCS; published in *On the proper Management of Vaccination, with the causes and prevention of its failure to protect the constitution from any after-influence of the contagion of Small Pox, with an additional paper on the infection of other diseases*, Berkeley 1843, 20 pp., at pp. 17–19. WHM has two copies, one inscribed by the author.

*Suggestions for the Treatment and Management of Tetanus, or Lockjaw.* Berkeley 1845.

George and Henry Jenner joined in a petition to Parliament in 1840 for reward of their long services to vaccination, but without result; the text was printed by Victor G. Plarr in 'The Twilight of the Jenners', *Medical Magazine*, February 1902.

CHAPTER 8

# Biographies, Dedications and Portraits

Edward Jenner: look at his carefully written pages – the beautiful portraits express the same thing, what a noble, kindly, generous man he was, modest and benevolent, with but the single thought in mind of wiping out of the world the greatest of all human plagues.

Henry Barton Jacobs, 1932.

## I   BIOGRAPHIES

John Baron's *Life of Edward Jenner* is the only large-scale biography by a man who knew him well. Thomas Pruen of Prestbury, who had known Jenner longer and perhaps more intimately than Baron, expected to be invited to write the official biography, but Jenner's family chose the physician who had worked with him in his later years. Baron included a very large selection from Jenner's correspondence, which gave immediacy to his narrative. In describing the controversies which beset Jenner's campaign for universal vaccination he wrote of persons and events but not of scientific questions, and did not trace the gradual development of Jenner's thought about the problems which arose as his knowledge of vaccination increased through practice. Baron emphasized the width of Jenner's interests and the respect and affection which he earned among eminent men beyond the circle of his neighbouring friends, but his record of Jenner's position and practice at Cheltenham was quite inadequate. His reading of Jenner's character, almost a hagiography, provoked extreme reaction among later critics.

Edgar Crookshank, professor of bacteriology at King's College, London in the 1880s, was the most influential of these critics. His scholarly *History and Pathology of Vaccination* (2 vols, 1889) included a 'Life and Letters of Edward Jenner' (vol. 1, chapters 6–8) and reprinted Jenner's principal publications. He believed, perhaps rightly, that the current

127

production of vaccine was unscientific and dangerous to health, laying the blame for this on faults which he exaggerated in Jenner's character and behaviour in controversy. About the same time Charles Creighton's profoundly learned *A History of Epidemics in Great Britain* (2 vols, 1891–94) debased Jenner's fame even lower. His account of smallpox (vol. 2, chapter 4) dismissed vaccination as unnecessary and ineffective, and criticized Jenner's work in detail; he had previously attacked Jenner in a separate book *Jenner and Vaccination* (1889). Sir Norman Moore, a prominent London physician and medical historian, helped to restore a balanced view of vaccination by his memoir of Jenner in the *Dictionary of National Biography* (vol. 29, 1892, pp. 321–4) when the *Dictionary* was establishing its position as the first authoritative British biographical encyclopaedia. Moore, however, in this memoir described Jenner's correct account of cuckoo behaviour as 'absurd', having learned his knowledge of birds from the eccentric anti-Jennerian naturalist Charles Waterton.

Determination of the nature of viruses by Dmitri Ivanovski in 1892, and the analysis of vaccines by Monckton Copeman, reported in his Milroy Lectures to the Royal College of Physicians on *Vaccination, its Natural History and Pathology* (1898) prepared the way for scientific re-assessment of Jenner's achievement, fully surveyed from the viewpoint of a virologist by Dr Derrick Baxby (1981). Two excellent summaries of Jenner's work and its influence on medical science as well as on public health were published in the *British Medical Journal* in 1949, at the bicentenary of his birth, by E. Ashworth Underwood, Director of the Wellcome Institute for the History of Medicine, and Sir Edward Mellanby, Secretary of the Medical Research Council. Jenner had failings and made mistakes, but he was not the charlatan portrayed by some critics even in the 1970s while vaccination was winning its complete victory over smallpox.

Biographies of Jenner and essays about him, with notices in every history of medicine, are very numerous, but it is uneconomic to print lists of all these, now that they can be traced readily through the computer-recorded catalogues of the great libraries, particularly the United States National Library of Medicine. Biographies published since 1951 include the following, the last two providing new information:

Dorothy Fisk *Dr. Jenner of Berkeley*. London 1959.

Edward F. Dolan *Jenner and the Miracle of Vaccination*. New York 1960.

A. J. Harding Rains *Edward Jenner and Vaccination*. London 1973.

W. R. LeFanu 'Edward Jenner', *Proceedings of the Royal Society of Medicine* 66 (1973), 664–68.

Leonard G. Wilson 'Jenner, Edward . . . natural history, immunology, medicine', *Dictionary of Scientific Biography*, New York 7 (1973), 95–97.

Derrick Baxby *Jenner's Smallpox Vaccine, the Riddle of Vaccine Virus and its Origin*. London 1981. [A history of the identification of animal pox viruses from Jenner's time to modern research in which the author has worked.]

Paul Saunders *Edward Jenner, the Cheltenham Years 1795–1823, being a Chronicle of the Vaccination Campaign*. Hanover, New Hampshire 1982. [Written from long familiarity with Cheltenham and its history, and wide research in local and other records.]

## BIOGRAPHIES BY JENNER'S CONTEMPORARIES

1  [Alexander Tilloch] 'Some account of Edward Jenner, M.D.', *Philosophical Magazine*, no. 51 (August 1802), 266–68, article 44: with engraving by Mackenzie of Smith's portrait.

2  Benjamin Waterhouse [Biographical account of Dr. Jenner] in his *A prospect of exterminating the smallpox*, part 2, Cambridge, New England 1802, Appendix pp. 135–39.

3  [John Ring] 'Dr. Jenner' in *Public Characters of 1802–3*. (London 1803) vol. 5, pp. 18–49, with stipple-engraved profile portrait, ascribed to Ring by Louis Valentin (no. 19 below).

4  John Coakley Lettsom 'Memoir of Edward Jenner, M.D. From Dr. Lettsom's Oration delivered before the Medical Society of London on March 8, 1804', *European Magazine*, 46 (September 1804), 163–66; with Ridley's engraving of Northcote's second portrait.

The same, separately printed by Bryan, Grocers' Hall Court, Poultry, 10 pp.

Again, printed by J. Gold, London, 7 pp.

The same, *Philadelphia Medical Magazine* 11 (1806), 445–61.

The same, in Samuel Agnew *A short practical Treatise on the Efficacy of Kinepox Inoculation*. Gettysburg, Pennsylvania 1806, 84 pp.

[French translation:] *Eloge d'Edouard Jenner prononcé en présence de la Société de Médecine de Londres*. Traduit par Joseph Duffour. Paris, Capelle et Renaud 1811. 46 pp.

5 Louis Valentin 'Notice biographique sur le Dr. Jenner', *Annales de Médecine clinique de Montpellier*, 5 (1805), and separately Montpellier, impr. Tournel. An XIII, 11 pp.

6 F. Bruni *Istruzioni del Comitato centrale di Vaccinazione [Firenze], precedute da alcune notizie istoriche sopra Eduardo Jenner*. Florence 1810.

7[6] 'The life of Dr. Jenner' *Analectic Magazine*, Philadelphia, 9 (January 1817), 48–59. Based on Lettsom's Memoir of 1804, with engraved portrait by R. M. Meadows after J. Robinson.

8 James Moore *The History and Practice of Vaccination*. London 1817.

9[7] Thomas Dudley Fosbroke 'Biographical Anecdotes of Edward Jenner, M.D., F.R.S.' in his *Berkeley Manuscripts – Abstracts and extracts of Smyth's Lives of the Berkeleys . . . history of the Castle and Parish of Berkeley . . . and Biographical Anecdotes of Dr. Jenner, his interviews with the Emperor of Russia, etc*. London John Nichols, 1821 at pp. 219–42; pedigree of Kingscote (including Edward Jenner, his wife and children), facing p. 218; pedigree of Jenner of Berkeley formerly Genor, facing p. 220.

10[8] [Anecdotes of the memorial to the King of Spain], *Gentleman's Magazine* May 1822, p. 396. See also no. **160** above.

11[9] John Baron 'Edward Jenner, Esq., M.D.', *Gloucester Journal*, 3 February 1823.

The same, reprinted as a broadsheet *Death of Dr. Jenner*, unsigned, 2 columns.

The same, *Gentleman's Magazine* 93 (February 1823), 179–81, with further passages not by Baron.

The same, *London Medical and Physical Journal* 49 (March 1823), 271–72, with three paragraphs by the editors and a list of Jenner's publications.

12[10]   [William Davies] 'Anecdotes of the late Dr. Jenner', *Gentleman's Magazine* 93 (February 1823), 104, signed W.D.

13   T. F. Dibdin 'Reminiscences of Dr. Jenner', *The Museum*, February 1823.

14[11]   [Henry Jenner] 'Of the late Dr. Jenner', *Gazette of Health* 8, (no. 93) (1 September 1823), 634–38, signed Z.Z.; the writer says that *Migration of Birds* was 'revised by Dr. Jenner with the Rev. G. C. Jenner and myself'.

15[12]   'Memoir of Jenner', *Imperial Magazine*, April 1823.

16[13]   'Dr. Jenner', *New Monthly Magazine*, London 9 (April 1823), 184–85; the writer had known and talked with Jenner.

17[14]   Christian Wilhelm Hufeland 'Edward Jenners Tod', *Journal der Heilkunde* 56 (March 1823), 127–28.

18[15]   Henri-Marie Husson 'Jenner', *Dictionnaire des Sciences médicales, Biographie médicale*, ed. J. L. Jourdan, Paris 5 (1822), 349–55; published after Jenner's death in January 1823; additions and corrections from Valentin's *Notice* (no. 19 following) on pp. 574–75.

19[16]   Louis Valentin *Notice historique sur le Docteur Jenner, suivie de Notes relatives à sa Découverte de la Vaccine*. Nancy, C. J. Hissette, 1823, 47 pp; 2me. edition 1824, 52 pp; also in *Précis de Travaux de la Société royale de Nancy* 1825, pp. 227–48.

20   'Dr. Jenner – a short biographical Sketch', *The Hive or Weekly Register*, London 1 (1823), no. 17.

21[17]   'Edward Jenner, Esq., M.D., LL.D., F.R.S., M.N.I.F. A Physician extraordinary to the King, and a Magistrate of the County of

Gloucester', *Annual Obituary*, London 1824, pp. 186–217; agrees in some detail with John Fosbroke's memoir (no. 26 below) and reprints Baron's obituary (no. 11 above).

22[18]   [Henry Jenner] 'Some observations on the Social Life and Character of the late Dr. Jenner, M.D., LL.D., etc. etc. By one of his most intimate Friends', *The Literary Magnet of the Belles Lettres, Science and the Fine Arts*, 1 (April 1824), 174–76; agrees with the obituary attributed to Henry Jenner (no. 14 above); [Danish translation:] 'Et Par Ord om Jenner's selskabelige Liv og Character', *Nye Hygaea*, Copenhagen 5 (January 1825), 68–75.

23[19]   Amédée Dupay *Notice historique sur le Docteur Edward Jenner, Inventeur de la Vaccine*, Paris, Rignoux 1824, 16 pp.; with bibliography by Baron, other material supplied by Valentin, and a portrait.

24[20]   'Memoir of Edward Jenner, M.D.', *The Portfolio*, Philadelphia 19 (1825), 512–15; with stipple-engraved portrait by R. M. Meadows after J. Robinson; based on Baron's obituary (no. 11 above).

25[21]   [John Knight] 'Dr. Edward Jenner', *Professional Anecdotes, or Ana of medical Literature*, London. John Knight and Henry Lacey (1825) 3 vols: Vol. 1, pp. 101–05 Dr. Edward Jenner; pp. 169–73 Jenner on the cuckoo; Vol. 2, facing p. 1, folded facsimile of letter from Jenner to R. Phillips, 16 January 1807; p. 69 Dr. Jenner; p. 74 Lines on the tomb of Dr. Jenner; facing p. 74 stipple portrait by W. Read; Vol. 3, pp. 13–14 Rapid progress of vaccination; pp. 57–58 Vaccination abroad; pp. 75–78 Jenner's public reward.

26[22]   John Fosbroke 'Local Biography. Dr. Jenner' in T. D. Fosbroke *A Picturesque and topographical Account of Cheltenham and its Vicinity, to which are added, Contributions towards the Medical Topography, including the medical history of the Waters by John Fosbroke*. Cheltenham, S. C. Harper, 1826, pp. 271–300.

John Fosbroke was Jenner's assistant in his Cheltenham practice.

27[23]   John Baron *The Life of Edward Jenner, M.D., LL.D., F.R.S., Physician Extraordinary to the King, etc. etc., with Illustrations of his Doctrines and Selections from his Correspondence*. London, Henry Colburn 1827, xxiv,

624 pp. Reissued with a cancel title-page 'In two volumes, vol. 1, 1838' with the new Vol. 2: *The Life of Edward Jenner, M.D., LL.D., F.R.S., Physician Extraordinary to His Majesty Geo. IV, Foreign Associate of the National Institute of France, . . .* vol. 11, London 1838, viii, 471 pp. Frontispiece portraits: Vol. 1, lithograph by R. J. Lane from a drawing of Manning's bust by H. Corbould: Vol. 2, W. H. Mote's stipple engraving of Lawrence's portrait, issued this year 1838 for Pettigrew's *Medical Portrait Gallery* (no. 31 below).

28[24] Johann Ludwig Choulant 'Edward Jenner', *Zeitgenossen, ein biographisches Magazin für die Geschichte unserer Zeit*, Leipzig, 3rd series, 1, no. 7 (1829), 3–42. Jenner's poem *Signs of rain* is included in English.

29[25] [Francis Bisset Hawkins] 'Jenner', in [William Macmichael] *Lives of British Physicians*. London, John Murray 1830, pp. 252–74; facing p. 252, line engraving by Edward Finden of Northcote's Plymouth portrait of Jenner. Bound (1) in red cloth with gilt lettering on spine; (2) in brown printed cloth, as no. XIV of *The Family Library*; second edition, London, Thomas Tegg 1846; third edition, London, William Tegg 1857.

30[26] Thomas Frognall Dibdin *Reminiscences of a Literary Life*. London, John Major, 1 (1836), 199–202: Reminiscences of Dr. Jenner with facsimile of Jenner's signature at p. 202. (See no. 13 above).

31[27] Thomas Joseph Pettigrew 'Edward Jenner, M.D., LL.D., F.R.S.' in his *Medical Portrait Gallery. Biographical Memoirs of the most celebrated Physicians, Surgeons, etc., etc., who have contributed to the Advancement of Medical Science*. London and Paris, 2, no. 10 [1838], 1–16, with stipple engraving by W. H. Mote of Sir Thomas Lawrence's portrait of Jenner; includes Pettigrew's personal recollections.

32[28] [Forbes Winslow] 'A sketch of the life of Dr. Edward Jenner', in his *Physic and Physicians*, London, 2 (1839), 71–81.

## II  Dedications

Many of Jenner's supporters dedicated their reports about vaccination to him. He was also flattered and entertained by gifts of verses in his honour, written or printed, which showed the wide diffusion of his discovery at home and abroad. The list which follows is arranged by date of publication.

1  Thomas Dudley Fosbroke *The Economy of Monastic Life, A Poem.* Gloucester, printed [1795?]. Dedicated in Gratitude to Edward Jenner.

2  Edward Gardner *Miscellanies in Prose and Verse.* Bristol, Biggs and Cottle 1798. Vol. 1, Prose, 41, 231 pp.; vol. 2, Verse, 31, 170 pp. Dedicated 'To Edward Jenner, M.D., F.R.S.'; at pp. 125 and 135 of vol. 2 are Sonnets to Edward Jenner.

3[2]  Thomas Paytherus *A Comparative Statement . . . relative to the Cowpox,* 1800 and 1801, dedicated to Jenner and Woodville. See **61 & 62** above.

4[3]  William Fermor *Reflections on the Cow-pox . . . in a Letter to Dr. Jenner.* London 1800. See Chapter 3, VIII.

5[4]  William Woodville *Observations on the Cow-pox.* London, William Phillips 1800, 43 pp.; dedicated 'To Edward Jenner, M.D., F.R.S., F.L.S. etc 1 July 1800'.

6  Jacques L. Moreau *Traité historique et pratique de la Vaccine.* Paris An IX 1801. 'A Edouard Jenner'; includes extracts from his writings, translated.

7  Georg Friedrich Ballhorn and Christian Friedrich Stromeyer *Traité de l'Inoculation de Vaccine, avec Observations faites à Hanover.* Leipzig 1801. Dedicated to Jenner and Jean de Carro.

8[5]  John Glover Loy *An Account of some Experiments on the Origin of the Cow-pox.* Whitby 1802. Dedicated 'To Edward Jenner . . . 13 October 1801'. Reprinted 1889 (Crookshank *History of Vaccination,* 2, 275 ff.); [French translation]: *Expériences sur l'Origine de la Vaccine . . . traduit par Jean de Carro. Avec quelques Observations du Traducteur et des Fragments de sa Correspondance avec le Docteur Jenner.* Vienna 1802.

9[6]   Benjamin Waterhouse *A Prospect of Exterminating the Smallpox.* Cambridge, New England 1800, 40 pp.; Part II, 1802, 139 pp.: 'To John Coakley Lettsom and to Edward Jenner'.

10   Luke Booker *A Discourse (addressed chiefly to parents) on the Duty and Advantage of inoculating Children with the Cow-pock.* London 1802 (2 editions); [a Sermon dedicated to Edward Jenner]. From Booker's letter to Jenner (Dudley, 17 March 1803, printed by Baron, 1, 592–93) he appears to have had a summary of his sermon printed as a leaflet, of which he distributed about twenty a week at baptisms.

11   John Redman Coxe *Practical Observations on Vaccination . . . Embellished with a coloured Engraving [Tanner sc.] representing [13] various stages of the Vaccine and Small-pox.* Philadelphia 1802. Dedicated to Edward Jenner, June 1st 1802.

12[7]   'Dr. Vivas of Valentia' *Epigramma* [four Latin couplets], quoted in *Public Characters* 1803, p. 49.

13[8]   Robert John Thornton *Facts decisive in Favour of the Cow-Pock.* London 1802; second and third issues 1803. Dedicated to Edward Jenner. The first issue included the first printing of Jenner's *Petition,* and later issues added the *Evidence* and *Report* of the Committee on Jenner's claim.

14   *Poetical Effusions from Fairy Camp,* Tewkesbury, W. Dyde 1803, 2 vols.; at vol. 2, pp. 120–22 Verses 'To Jenner, Oct. 5, 1800 by An Amateur' [By Powell Snell.] Cheltenham Reference Library; Saunders (1982) 93 and 436.

15[9]   I. Brandon 'Address to Dr. Jenner' [at the first 'anniversary celebration' of his birthday by the Royal Jennerian Society], *Gentleman's Magazine* 1803; separate issue inscribed 'From the Author', among John Baron's Jenner papers at RCS.

Reprinted 1820 (BL).

16[10]   Christopher Anstey *Ad Edvardum Jenner . . . carmen alcaicum.* London and Bath 1803; twenty-three Latin alcaic stanzas of which Baron (1, 598–99) quoted nine; *Ode to Edward Jenner* [translation by John Ring] 1804, and in *Gentleman's Magazine* 75 (1805), 325–26.

135

17[11]   Thomas Alston Warren [*A Poem*, circa 1803]. Baron reports (1, 600) that Warren sent Jenner a poem when sending his *An Address from a Country Minister to his Parishioners on the Subject of the Cow-pox or Vaccine Inoculation*. London, Bye and Law [for the Royal Jennerian Society], 1803. 16 pp. A copy of the address and a copy of its fifth edition (Nichols and Son 1805) are among Baron's papers at RCS, but there is no poem.

18[12]   Robert Bloomfield *Good Tidings, or News from the Farm, Ode recited at the Anniversary Meeting of the Royal Jennerian Society 1804*. London 1804. 'Dedicated to Edward Jenner, as the Discoverer, and to the Members of the Royal Jennerian Society, as the Promoters of the Vaccine inoculation'.

19[13]   Thomas Trotter *An Essay, medical, philosophical, and chemical, on Drunkenness, and its Effects on the Human Body*. London, Longman and Rees 1804, 203 pp.; second edition 1804; etc. The dedication to Dr Jenner is dated 26 December 1803. Trotter introduced vaccination into the Royal Navy; in 1801 he organized the presentation of a medal from the Naval Surgeons to Jenner, an illustration of which appears as frontispiece to his *Medicina Nautica*, vol. 3, 1803. See I. A. Porter 'Thomas Trotter', *Medical History* 7 (1963), 155–64.

20[14]   James Plumtre [*Two Sermons on Numb. lx, 48* 'He stood between the dead and the living, and the plague was stayed', Feb. 1805 University Sermon; March 1805 'simple' Sermon at Hinxton], Cambridge 1805; dedication to Jenner quoted in full by Baron (2, 41–2 n). Verses in praise of vaccination, 'printed and circulated' by Plumtre are quoted in T. J. Pettigrew *Lettsom* 1817, vol. 2, Appendix. See also Saunders (1983) pp. 165–66 and 448 n. 39.

21[15]   John Coakley Lettsom 'Verses on Jenner' at third festival of the Royal Jennerian Society, 17 May 1805. *Gentleman's Magazine* 75 (1805), 523.

22   John Davis *The First Settlers of Virginia* [a novel], 1805; 2nd ed. 1806. Dedication to Jenner dated New York, January 1806. Davis was in England in 1804 when Jenner wrote to him accepting his proposed dedication and mentioning Benjamin Waterhouse and 'my public advertisement in some of the Continental papers' (see no. **76**). (Information from Whitfield J. Bell, Jr, Philadelphia.)

23   T. P. [Thomas Pruen] *Vaccinia, or the Triumph of beauty, A Poem.* London 1806: 'To Jenner's name a grateful world shall raise / The well-earned monument of deathless praise'. (Attributed wrongly to Thomas Paytherus in my first edition 1951; correct information from Anthony Lister, Sandbach, Cheshire).

24[16]   Jacob Lodewijk Kesteloot *Immortali Jennero* [Latin poem]. Rotterdam 1807.

25[17]   William Blair *Hints for the Consideration of Parliament in a Letter to Dr. Jenner 28–31 March 1808.* London, J. Callow 1808. Running title: A letter to Dr. Jenner in reply to Mr. Birch. John Birch published objections to vaccination in 1805, 1806 and 1807 and again later.

COPY: RCS inscribed 'From the author'.

26[18]   John Dawes Worgan *An Address to the Royal Jennerian Society 1808; Select poems, etc., by the late John Dawes Worgan of Bristol, who died on July 25, 1809, Aged Nineteen with Particulars of his life and character.* London, Longman 1810. Dedication to Edward Jenner; at pp. 184–91 Latin ode on vaccination; pp. 201–11 'Address' of 1808 and 'Essays on Vaccination' from *Gentleman's Magazine* 1808–09. Worgan had been tutor to Jenner's sons, see Samuel Wood 'A Link with Jenner', *Annals of Medical History*, 8 (1936), 433–41.

27[19]   Gioachino Ponta *Il Trionfo della Vaccinia.* Parma 1810. The verses referring to Jenner are quoted by Baron (*2*, 172–73).

28[20]   John Williams *Sacred Allegories . . . to which is added An Anacreontic on Vaccination with an Epilogue addressed to Dr. Jenner.* London, Longman 1810. See Saunders (1983) pp. 256–57, an account of the author.

29[21]   Christian Wilhelm Hufeland 'Rede zur Feier des Tages an welchem Eduard Jenner zuerst die Schutzpocken einimpfte, nebst einem Nachtrag', *Asklepieion*, 2 (May 1811), 657–68.

30   T. D. Fosbroke *An Ode to Hygeia on the Vaccine Inoculation* [1811]. (Baron *2*, 174).

31[22]   Jakob Johan Walop *Hulde aan Eduard Jenner en allen die zich, door de vorbreiding en bevordering die koepok-inenting, aan de menschheid hebben vordienstelijk gemaakt*. Rotterdam 1812.

32[23]   S. Dobell *A floweret for the wreath of humanity, with other pieces in verse* . . . 1812; at p. 29 Eulogium on Dr. Jenner.

33   Thomas Baynton *An Account of a successful Method of treating Diseases of the Spine*. London, Longman 1813. Dedicated to Edward Jenner.

34[24]   William Gardiner *Poems on various occasions*. Gloucester, D. Walker 1813; at pp. 41–44 Ode to Dr. Jenner; *Enlarged edition, with Memoir by his daughter*, 1854; includes Jenner's letter to Gardiner of 27 September 1812.

35[25]   Caleb Hillier Parry *Cases of Tetanus; and Rabies contagiosa, or Canine Hydrophobia*. Bath and London 1814; dedication 'To Edward Jenner . . . Bath, July 26, 1814', in which Parry described Jenner as his friend during nearly fifty years.

36[26]   James Moore *The History of the Smallpox*, London, Longman 1815; dedicated 'To Edward Jenner, M.D., F.R.S., etc. etc.'; second edition 1818.

37[27]   P. Py 'La Découverte de la Vaccine'. Narbonne 1816. A manuscript poem presented to Jenner, and quoted by Baron (2, 174). Wellcome MS 2086.

38   Sebastien Guillie *An Essay on the Instruction and Amusement of the Blind*, from the French. London 1819; dedicated to Jenner by the translator.

39   William S. Wickenden *Count Glarus of Switzerland*. London 1819; 'Dedicated by permission to Edward Jenner M.D.'.

40[28]   John Baron *Illustrations of the Enquiry respecting Tubercular Diseases*. London (Gloucester printed) 1822. The dedication copy, with Jenner's autograph notes, is in the British Library.

41[29]   F. van der Breggen *Feestviering ter huldigung van Edward Jenner en ter verheffing van der waardij der koepokinenting, van wegen het genootschap Arti Salutiferae te Amsterdam gehouden de xiv Mei 1823.* Amsterdam 1823.

42[30]   T. D. Fosbroke *Masonic Jennerian Sermon, preached in the Cathedral of Gloucester, August 19, 1823, in aid of the Subscription for erecting a Monument in honour of Dr. Jenner, before the Provincial Grand Lodges of the Counties of Gloucester and Hereford.* Gloucester 1823.

43[31]   J. B. G. Camberlyn-d'Amongies *Jennero.* Gand 1824, [a Latin poem].

44[32]   Robert Southey *A Tale of Paraguay*, 1823; stanzas 1–3 refer to Jenner.

45[33]   Thomas Frognall Dibdin *Reminiscences . . .* 1836; at p. 200 Dibdin recalls that he had written a poem in blank verse entitled *Vaccinia* 'but all traces of it are lost'.

46   William S. Wickenden *Poems and Tales*, London 1851, dedicated to Edward Jenner.

47[34]   M. W. Luber and W. H. Warnsinck *Het vijftigjarig bestaan van het Amsterdamsche Genootshap ter bevordering der Koepokinenting voor minvermogenden herdacht op November 1, 1853.* Amsterdam 1853; at pp. 36–38 a poem to Jenner.

## III   PORTRAITS

Jenner's friend Edward Gardner described him as he appeared in early middle age: 'His height was rather under the middle size, his person was robust, but active and well-formed. In his dress he was peculiarly neat, and everything about him showed the man intent and serious, and well prepared to meet the duties of his calling. When I first saw him it was on Frampton Green. I was somewhat his junior in years, and had heard so much of Mr. Jenner of Berkeley, that I had no small curiosity to see him. He was dressed in a blue coat and yellow buttons, buckskins, well-polished jockey boots, with handsome silver spurs, and he carried a smart whip with a silver handle. His hair, after the fashion of the times, was done up in a club, and he wore a broad-brimmed hat'.

Many portraits exist, and we have his own and other contemporary opinions of some of them. The most familiar, which shows him leaning against a tree, is probably the earliest, painted by J. R. Smith in 1800 when Jenner was fifty. James Northcote painted him in 1802 and again in 1803. These three pictures show him as a solid, broad-faced man of open countenance. About the same time Samuel Medley added a portrait of Jenner into the group which he had already completed of the principal members of the Medical Society of London. Sir Thomas Lawrence painted him in 1809; the face is somewhat idealized, with features less blunt. When he was seventy-two he was painted by William Hobday; this picture shows him grown heavier.

Jenner wrote to Lettsom in 1804 that 'Smith's is a strange likeness, but neither [he nor Northcote] have succeeded in giving my character. Smith's with a few careless touches from the engraver degenerates into an assassin'. In 1810, after Lawrence had painted him, Jenner still thought Northcote's first portrait the best; in 1804 he had praised Say's engraving of it. Lettsom preferred Medley's painting to Smith's, and said that 'Jenner entertained a favourable opinion of it'. Baron praised the bust exhibited by Charles Manning at the Royal Academy in 1805 as 'an extremely faithful and valuable likeness, a most satisfactory resemblance'; of this bust Jenner gave away replicas. Baron wrote of Northcote's first portrait: 'It wants the peculiar expression of Jenner's countenance and does not fully display his manner, but on the whole it is a better portrait than some which have appeared since'. He reported that the pencil drawing by J. B. Drayton, done from the life in 1805, 'is allowed to be one of the most exact resemblances of Dr. Jenner'. Louis Valentin, who knew Jenner well, somewhat surprisingly describes the engraving made after Smith's portrait by P. Anderloni of Milan for a frontispiece to L. Sacco's *Trattato di vaccinazione* 1809 as 'parfaitement rassemblant'.

There are portraits at Berkeley in the Castle and the Jenner Museum, and at Bristol City Art Gallery, whose provenance has not been fully reported; others of doubtful likeness include an oil painting given to the Royal College of Surgeons of England in 1887 and a pastel by John Russell RA sold at Christie's on 1 August 1957. After Jenner's death the statue which stands in Gloucester Cathedral was commissioned from Robert William Sievier (1825), and the statue in Kensington Gardens, London from William Calder Marshall RA (1858). There are also contemporary caricatures and other posthumous sculptures and paintings.

In the list which follows I record only portraits from the life, with an early engraving of each; these engravings are referenced to the Wellcome Institute Catalogue: *Portraits of Doctors and Scientists in the Wellcome Institute of the History of Medicine, A Catalogue*, by Renate Burgess, London 1973, which lists two original and forty-three engraved portraits of Jenner (no. 1527:1–45). There are useful lists in other catalogues of medical portraits and medals, besides the following special books and articles:

J. M. P. Munaret *Iconautographie de Jenner* 1860.

C. L. H. Kluyskens, 'Numismatique Jennerienne', *Revue belge de Numismatique*, 31 (1875), 55.

L. Pfeiffer 'Impfung Denkmünzen', *Deutsche Zeitschrift für praktische Medizin*, (1876), pp. 516–24.

C. Ruland 'Zu Ehren Jenner und Sacco Medaillen', *Archiv für pathologische Anatomie*, 62 (1877), 1–14.

L. Pfeiffer und C. Ruland *Pestilentia in Nummis*, Weimar 1880; Tübingen 1882.

L. Pfeiffer *Zur Jennerfeier*, Tübingen 1896.

H. R. Storer 'The memorials of Edward Jenner', *Journal of the American Medical Association*, 26 (1896), 312–17.

V. O. Hubert [*Small-pox and vaccination*], St Petersburg 1896.

'Portraits of Jenner', *British Medical Journal*, 1 (1896), 1257–60.

'Statues of Jenner in England', *British Medical Journal*, 2(1913), 1601.

D. Baxby 'An unusual portrait of Edward Jenner . . .' [engraving by A. M. Monsaldi, Paris, about 1812. (Wellcome 31)], *Medical History* 22 (1978), 335–39.

## PORTRAITS FROM THE LIFE
### (*In chronological order*)

**1  John Raphael Smith**

Three-quarter length, nearly full-face, standing against a tree with right arm on branch; in background, a view of Berkeley with cows and a milkmaid. Jenner wears a cut-away coat and striped waistcoat, hat in left hand.

*(i)* Pastel exhibited at Royal Academy, 1800: Wellcome Institute (1527–1); pastel replica in Cushing collection, Yale Medical Historical Library; replica, or early copy, in oils in Jacobs collection, Johns Hopkins University, Institute of the History of Medicine, Baltimore.

*(ii)* Mezzotint by the artist and his assistant William Ward (Wellcome 2).

**2  John Miers**

Silhouette, engraved for Lettsom, *Observations on the cow pock* (Wellcome 24).

**3  James Northcote**

First portrait: three-quarter length to right, but the face turned towards the left, seated, legs crossed, in fur-edged coat and double-breasted waistcoat; right hand on open book showing illustration of vaccine pustules.

*(i)* Oil, painted 1802, in the possession of the Plymouth Medical Society.

*(ii)* Oil, a copy from Northcote's studio, in the possession of the Devonport (Royal Albert) Hospital, Plymouth. These two portraits were exhibited, by the courtesy of the owners, at the National Portrait Gallery, London for the bicentenary celebration of Jenner's birth in May 1949.

*(iii)* Mezzotint by W. Say, 1804 (Wellcome 29).

**4  Samuel Medley**

*(i)* Oil, at Medical Society of London, added about 1802 to the group-portrait painted in 1800.

*(ii)* Stipple by N. Branwhite; the plate was engraved in 1801 without Jenner's figure, which was inserted later. (See Wellcome 2742.4.)

**5  W. Read**

*(i)* Pencil drawing, not signed.

*(ii)* Line engraving by W. Read [before 1803] (Wellcome 25).

6   *James Northcote*
Second portrait: three-quarter length, nearly full-face, seated, legs not crossed, in black suit; head rests on left hand, pen in right hand; open book, showing the 'sacred cow', propped up on table.
*(i)*  Oil, painted 1803, in the National Portrait Gallery.
*(ii)*  Stipple, by W. Ridley, 1804 (Wellcome 33).

7   *J. B. Drayton*
*(i)*  Pencil drawing, 1805.
*(ii)*  Line engraving by Anker Smith 1823 (Wellcome 27).

8   *Charles Manning*
*(i)*  Bust exhibited at Royal Academy 1805.
*(ii)*  Lithograph by R. J. Lane from Henry Corbould's drawing 1827 (Wellcome 43).

9   *John Hazlitt*
*(i)*  Miniature.
*(ii)*  Mezzotint by Charles Turner 1808 (Wellcome 28).

10   *Sir Thomas Lawrence*
Half-length to left, seated, in high-collared coat, with white cravat.
*(i)*  Oil, Painted 1809: Royal College of Physicians.
*(ii)*  Stipple by W. H. Mote 1838 (Wellcome 36).

11   *J. Robinson*
*(i)*  Miniature.
*(ii)*  Stipple by R. M. Meadows, 1817.

12   *William Hobday*
Three-quarter length, seated by table, left arm resting on a book by John Hunter.
*(i)*  Oil, painted 1821: Royal Society of Medicine, where also Jenner's autograph verses to the artist are in the Library.
*(ii)*  Line engraving begun by W. Sharp, completed by W. Skelton 1826 (Wellcome 38).

13   *Henry Edridge*
Pencil drawing, about 1821: Wellcome Institute (Wellcome 39 with reproduction).

14   *Stephen Jenner*
Coloured drawing, about 1819–22: Yale Medical Historical Library, Cushing collection.

# Notes

## Chapter 1

### I    BANKS'S SOUTH SEA SPECIMENS

H. B. Carter, J. A. Diment, C. J. Humphries and A. Wheeler 'The Banksian Natural History collections of the *Endeavour* voyage . . .', *History in the Service of Systematics*, Society for the Bibliography of Natural History, Special Publication 1 (1981), 61–70; P. J. P. Whitehead 'Zoological specimens from Captain Cook's voyages', *Journal of the Society for the Bibliography of Natural History*, 5 (1969), 161–201; and 'A guide to the dispersal of zoological material from Captain Cook's voyages', *Pacific Studies*, Hawaii, Fall 1978, pp. 72–93. In 1983 my daughter Mrs Nicola Lumsdaine searched through Banks's papers concerning his project of sailing with a staff of scientists in Cook's second voyage to the South Pacific in the Mitchell Library, Sydney, but found no mention of Jenner.

Hunter's Letters to Jenner: Baron *1*, 28–104; Ottley pp. 58–117.

Jenner's record of experiments: Baron *1*, 29.

### II    HIBERNATION

John Hunter 'Experiments on animals and vegetables with respect to the power of producing heat', *Philosophical Transactions* 65, (1778), 446–58; 'Of the heat of animals and vegetables', *Philosophical Transactions* 68, (1779), 7–49.

### III    THE FREE MARTIN

T. R. Forbes 'An early record [1768] of a free-martin' [referring also to Malpighi 1692], *Journal of the History of Medicine* 34 (1979) 355–56; Hunter's paper sent to Jenner: Ottley p. 75; Jenner to Worthington: Baron *2*, 409.

### IV    EMETIC TARTAR

Hunter to Jenner: Ottley pp. 86, 90–2.

### V    OPHTHALMIA

Baron *1*, 46 and 405; Ottley pp. 91 and 103.

VI   THE BOTTLENOSED WHALE

Royal College of Surgeons, Hunterian Museum *Descriptive Catalogue of the Physiological Series*, part I (1970), nos. 740 and 742; part II (1971) no. 3742.

VII   THE JACKAL

John Hunter 'Wolf, Jackal and Dog', *Philosophical Transactions* 77 (1787), 253 and 79 (1789), 160.

X   THE CUCKOO

Jenner to Banks, June 1787, and Banks to Jenner 7 July 1787; these letters refer also to *Fox and Dog* and *Animal Manures*: Baron *1*, 73–77 and 77–78; W. R. Dawson *The Banks Letters, A Calendar*, British Museum (Natural History) 1958, p. 474 Jenner to Banks 28 December 1787; Dawson 'Banks . . . supplementary Letters, 2nd series', *Bulletin of the British Museum (Natural History), Historical series*, 3 (1965), 83 Jenner to Banks, June 1787 (misdated 1789), and p. 84 Banks to Jenner, 7 July 1787 (summary inaccurate).

Jenner's first and second drafts of Cuckoo paper: Royal Society Archives, LP 9, 37 and 80.

Hunter to Jenner, May 1788: Baron *1*, 78.

Jenner's dissections: Royal College of Surgeons, Hunterian Museum *Descriptive Catalogue of the Physiological Series*, part I (1970) no. 534; part II (1971) nos. 3376 A and B.

Vernacular bird names: Jenner did not use the Linnean names, but they were added in the French and Italian translations.

F. H. Lancum [The eviction process], *Proceedings of the Linnean Society*, 142 (1929–30), 25.

J. S. Huxley 'On the relation between egg-weight and body-weight', *Journal of the Linnean Society (Zoology)*, 36 (1927), 457–66.

Ian Wyllie *The Cuckoo* London, Batsford, 1981. cf. Drewitt, no. **146**, p. 7.

Lawrence Kilham 'Edward Jenner, pioneer student of two major ornithological problems', *The Auk*, 90 (1973), 752–58.

XI   MEDICAL RESEARCHES: HEART DISEASE, SMALLPOX ETC.

W. C. Wells 'On rheumatism of the heart', *Transactions of the Society for the Improvement of Medical and Chirurgical Knowledge* 3 (1812), 373–424; the paper had been read on 3 April 1810.

Jenner to Parry, 10 January 1805: *Letters . . . Jacobs collection*, ed. G. Miller 1983, no. 17.

W. Heberden, *Medical Transactions of the Royal College of Physicians* 2 (1772), 59–67 and 3 (1785), 1–11.

Hunter to Jenner, 11 May 1777: Baron *1*, 36; Jenner to Heberden: Baron *1*, 39–40.

Everard Home to Jenner, 18 February 1794: Baron *1*, 104–5.

Sir Thomas Lewis, 'Caleb Hillier Parry', *Cardiff Medical Society Proceedings* (1940), 71–89.

Brian Livesley, 'The resolution of the Heberden-Parry controversy', *Medical History*, 19 (1975), 158–71.

## Chapter 2

### THE COWPOX INQUIRY

Heading quotation: Sir L. Whitby *British Medical Journal* 2, (1948), 3.

Jenner to Gardner, 19 July 1796: Baron *1*, 137–8; facsimiles *Lancet* 27 June 1896 and LeFanu, *Bio-Bibliography* 1951, Plates 28–29.

Everard Home to Banks 21 April 1797: W. R. Dawson *The Banks Letters* 1958, p. 419: Home no. 9, the autograph is in the library of the Royal Botanic Gardens, Kew.

Disappearance of cowpox during 1797: Baron *1*, 140; Saunders (1982), 52.

Anaphylaxis: F. Magendie *Lectures on the Blood*, [Paris], Philadelphia 1839, 244–49; P. Portier and C. Richet *Comptes rendus de la Société de Biologie de Paris*, 54 (1902), 170–2; Clemens von Pirquet, *Münchener medizinische Wochenschrift* 53 (1906), 1457 and *Klinische Studien über Vakzination und Vakzinale Allergie*, Vienna 1907 (autograph in Wellcome Institute Library, MS 3909).

Manuscripts of *Inquiry*: D. Baxby, *Medical History* 24 (pt. 2) (April 1985).

Thomas Bradley's review of *Inquiry*: *Medical and Physical Journal*, 1 (1799), 1–11.

James Blake Bailey, criticism of Crookshank: *British Medical Journal*, 1 (1896), 1257.

Derrick Baxby's discussion of the *Inquiry*: Baxby (1981) chapter 5, pp. 52–69.

## Chapter 3

### VACCINATION

VI SEPARATE COWPOX ILLUSTRATIONS

John Christie McVail, 'Cowpox and smallpox', *British Medical Journal* 1 (1896), 1271–6: at pp. 1275–76 [Early illustrations, with reproductions of Kirtland's drawings]. Reginald Fitz, *Bulletin of the History of Medicine*, 11 (1942), 256, fig. 5. George Dock, *New York Medical Journal*, 76 (1902), 978.

IX INSTRUCTIONS

**76**, note: Jenner to Waterhouse, 24 February 1802: Baron *1*, 595.

David Ramsay, 22 July 1802: Miller (1983). Appendix: Letter 2.

XII EVIDENCE

Jenner's two awards: Baron *1*, 484–510 and 2, 556–59; Saunders (1982) pp. 115 and 203.

Hunter's cowpox drawing: Ottley, 39.

Hicks's Answer to Pearson: Baron *1*, 519.

Jenner to Spalding, 10 November 1801: J. A. Spalding *Dr. Lyman Spalding* 1916, 94–95.

C. Murray *Debates . . .* 1808: Copy at Cambridge University Library, Dr Richard Hunter's collection.

XIII VACCINATION AT BRISTOL

Saunders (1982) pp. 116–17.

XVII LETTER TO LOUIS VALENTIN

Baron *1*, 586–87.

XVIII LETTERS FROM JEAN DE CARRO

Vaccine against plague: Baron *2*, 12–13.

XIX VARIETIES AND MODIFICATIONS

Baxby (1981), 134–49, Chapter 10: True and Spurious Cow-pox.

XXII DISTEMPER

Baron *1*, 450; Abernethy: information (1948) from John L. Thornton, Librarian, St Bartholomew's Hospital Medical College, extracted from the Abernethian Society's manuscript minute book.

XXV LETTER TO DILLWYN

Lord Lansdowne to Jenner 18 November 1806: Baron *2*, 77–78.

XXVI CIRCULAR LETTER

**119**. Saunders 1982, p. 415.

## Chapter 4

MEDICAL DIGRESSIONS

I CLASSES OF INTELLECT

Saunders (1982), 201–02 and 408.

II LETTER TO C. H. PARRY

Jenner to Edward Davies 1821: Wellcome Institute Library.

Jenner's letter, 5 December 1821: Dr Max Thorek's collection 1950, bought from M. Benjamin's catalogue (New York) no. 63.

Jenner to Charles Parry 27 December 1821: Duke University Medical Center Library, Durham, North Carolina; *Journal of the History of Medicine* 19 (1964), 69.

Jenner to John Nichols, 1 January 1822: Sotheby's sale 6 November 1951.

## Chapter 5

POSTHUMOUS WORKS

I MIGRATION OF BIRDS

Jenner to Shrapnell: Baron *1*, 114.

Thornbury to Jenner 22 March 1795: Baron *1*, 109–10.

Jenner to Blumenbach, September 1801: Baron *1*, 467.

L. Kilham, *The Auk* 90 (1973), 755–58, quoted above in Chapter 1, Section X, 'The Cuckoo', where the Hunterian Museum specimens are also listed, but the rook specimen was destroyed in 1941.

IV R. C. P. NOTEBOOK

Hunter to Jenner 8 December 1790: Baron *1*, 98.

Jenner to Worthington 13 December 1809: Baron *2*, 407.

## Chapter 6

LETTERS

E. H. Cornelius and A. J. Harding Rains, *Letters from the Past, John Hunter to Edward Jenner*, Royal College of Surgeons 1976.

LeRoy Crummer, *Annals of Medical History* 1(1929), 403.

Genevieve Miller, editor *Letters of Edward Jenner*, . . . *Jacobs Collection*, Baltimore 1983.

S. W. Mitchell *Transactions of the College of Physicians of Philadelphia* 22 (1900), 110–11.

P. W. van der Pass, *Janus* 51 (1964), 202.

Waterhouse to Jenner about President Jefferson: Baron *1*, 595.

Indian Chiefs to Jenner: *Edinburgh Medical and Surgical Journal*, 8(1812), 247; Baron *2*, 101.

*Chapter 8*

III  PORTRAITS

Descriptions of portraits: Baron *1*, 15, 395; *2*, 76, 97, 335 and 365.

Anderloni's engraving: L. Valentin *Voyage en Italie*, 2nd edition 1826, p. 291.

# Index